# Take Three Birds

# Take Three Birds

**Jilli Lime-Holt**

© Copyright Jilli Lime-Holt 2014

TAKE THREE BIRDS

All rights reserved.

The right of Jilli Lime-Holt to be identified as the author of this work has been asserted in accordance with the Copyright, Designs and Patents Act 1988.

No part of this publication may be reproduced, stored in a retrieval system, or transmitted, in any form or by any means, electronic, mechanical, photocopying, recording or otherwise, nor translated into a machine language, without the written permission of the publisher.

Condition of sale

This book is sold subject to the condition that it shall not, by way of trade or otherwise, be lent, re-sold, hired out or otherwise circulated in any form of binding or cover other than that in which it is published and without a similar condition including this condition being imposed on the subsequent purchaser.

ISBN 978-1-50335-566-8

# Contents

| | |
|---|---|
| Chapter One Hatching an Idea | 1 |
| Chapter Two The Early Birds | 5 |
| Chapter Three A Third Bird | 15 |
| Chapter Four All of a Twitter | 28 |
| Chapter Five Bird Watching | 39 |
| Chapter Six Feathering Nests | 53 |
| Chapter Seven Taking Flight | 72 |
| Chapter Eight Close Encounters of the Bird Kind | 83 |
| Chapter Nine Migrating Birds | 91 |
| Chapter Ten Pecking Order | 108 |
| Chapter Eleven Twittering On | 117 |
| Chapter Twelve Home to Roost | 134 |
| Chapter Thirteen Birds of a Feather | 151 |
| Chapter Fourteen Pecking Things Over | 159 |
| Chapter Fifteen Feathered Friends Forever? | 167 |
| About the authors | 180 |

*To Authonomy.com – where we all first met*

Editor's Note: This book contains some use of the word 'feck'. Some readers may worry this is just a soft form of an offensive word. It is not intended to be taken as such. In 2008 the Advertising Standards Authority (ASA) ruled that a poster for Magners Irish Cider which contained the phrase 'Feck off bees' was not offensive and unlikely to be taken as a swearword but as a mild rebuff. It is a word in frequent colloquial use in Ireland. In the context of this book it is not intended to give offence.

# Chapter One
# Hatching an Idea

**Facebook – via Private Message**

*Jilli: I've had a brilliant idea!*

*Tottie: <groan> Why does that announcement fill me with trepidation?*

*Jilli: No, really, something that might make us a bit of money.*

*Tottie: Now you have my attention. What?*

*Jilli: We could write a book.*

*Tottie: I think you'll find that's been done, you daft Doris.*

*Jilli: No, write one between us. The three of us, you, me and Posh Bird. About meeting up on Facebook and really getting on.*

*Tottie: I think that's probably been done.*

*Jilli: No, but people who might not have met in real*

*life and then find they really get on and become like best friends. And then, here's the twist, they're from three different countries, then they all meet up in one country.*

*Tottie: It would have to be France. You know I never leave the Auvergne.*

*Jilli: Fab! I don't go anywhere either, I get homesick at the end of my drive but I could come to you and Posh could too, we could all meet there.*

*Tottie: Helluva long way for you to drive on your own though. Why doesn't Posh fly out to you then you both come together? Bit of a road trip on the way, like Thelma and Louise. Just don't drive near any canyons.*

*Jilli: Then we all write exactly what we think of one another.*

*Tottie: This could all end in tears.*

*Jilli: It will be brill! It's not been done before like this.*

*Tottie: Sort of chick lit meets reality. Chickality? Is that a genre? Bloody good idea, Doris. Well done, Bird.*

*Jilli: Not such a daft Doris with this idea. I'll ask Posh Bird, hang on ...*

**five minutes later**

*Jilli: She's in – we're on!!*

# HATCHING AN IDEA

**a few weeks later …**

*Jilli: Posh is out, family stuff.*

*Tottie: I know, you daft Doris, I was in on the same PM. Shame, but obviously family stuff has to come before friend stuff.*

*Jilli: Shall we still do it?*

*Tottie: We need another bird on board. Bit flat with just the two of us. Invent another bird and make it part fiction?*

*Jilli: I really want to keep it real. We must know another writer who would fit in, from all the writer groups we belong to.*

*Tottie: Needs to be someone we can trust. Someone who isn't just going to nick the idea and run with it and get a book out before we do.*

*Jilli: We could sue them for copyright.*

*Tottie: There's no copyright in an idea, Doris. Who do we know we can trust?*

*Jilli: We can trust Janet.*

*Tottie: Which Janet?*

*Jilli: Janet Farmer*

*Tottie: Janet as in Farmer Bird Janet? Wowser, good idea, Bird. We could certainly trust her. Wonder if she'd be up for it?*

*Jilli: You know her better than I do. Ask her. But does she have a sense of humour?*

*Tottie: Is the Pope a catholic?*

*Jilli: Oh yeah, course, I forgot she's from Yorkshire.*
*Tottie: Don't say that, Bird, you'll start a new War of the Roses!! She's from Derbyshire.*

*Jilli: Close enough! Ask her, see what she thinks, though is she a young sixty-something like you or an old biddy? I need someone who can share driving to France!*

*Tottie: Feck, woman, she builds drystone walls for a living!!! She could pick your car up and run with it. But what if we all fall out? She's a farmer so she knows how to use a shotgun!! OK, I'll ask her ...*

**five minutes later ...**

*Tottie: I asked her. She's in. She's just ordering her passport. Take Three Birds it is!*

# Chapter Two
# The Early Birds

Jilli (Doris Bird) – Italy

I am known in the 'triangle' as Doris, probably because when anyone does something daft I refer to them as a 'Doris' and when it comes to computer stuff I am a proper Doris, so the name seems to have stuck. My real name is Jilli, I am forty-seven, but only first thing in the morning, the rest of the time I am about twenty-six. I live in Italy in a rural mountain village in the Apennines and I love it. I am a very happy, positive, optimistic person who always sees what she has got, and never worries about what she hasn't got.

I was brought up in a pub in Holmfirth in rural Yorkshire. Yorkshire is a beautiful green county in England. People born there are known for speaking their own dialect and are sometimes known as 'Tykes'.

My parents moved into The Butchers Arms on the 31st August 1967 and I was born on the 3rd September. They had two other children under the age of six, so moving house and taking on a new business must have been a challenge. When people ask me where I get my spirit and drive from I can only reply my 'my fantastic, crazy parents'.

My kids are the one thing I am really proud of. I remember as a teenager saying I don't want a job, I just want to get married and have babies. I went to school once, but didn't like it so came home at lunch time, deciding I didn't need an education to fulfil my dream - what a muppet!

I spent as little time in school as possible and the day of release was the best day of my life. I had a job within two weeks and never looked back.

I met my first boyfriend at fifteen, married him at twenty, divorced him at twenty-three; I wanted babies, he wanted beer. We were very much in love but he wasn't ready for all that responsibility. The thought of babies, bigger mortgage payments and becoming a fully fledged grown up at twenty absolutely terrified him. He took to the pub and I started hating him for it.

Six months after the end of my marriage I met my second boyfriend, and, not learning from previous mistakes I married that one as well, but not until I'd had two children with him, so at least I didn't rush in. Then a year after the marriage our daughter Millie arrived.

Little did I know at the time that the day before he married me he'd asked one of the neighbours to run away with him. He is now married to said neighbour. I am glad she said no the first time as I wouldn't have my lovely daughter but I really wish she'd taken him sooner. I wasted a lot of years on that tosser but am happy to say I escaped eventually.

I have been very lucky in the baby department in that every time I decided I wanted a baby I was pregnant within two weeks. I have had many friends and family members who suffered fertility problems and I cannot imagine how I would have handled it.

Long before I got pregnant, I knew I would not want a hospital birth, and I also knew I didn't want any drugs. When I announced to family and friends that I would be having a birthing pool in my kitchen I was met with all sorts of questions and comments. I don't think anybody believed I would do it.

I just kept telling them, 'It won't take long, and it won't

hurt'. I was half right; my first labour was one hour twenty minutes from my waters breaking to cuddling the little chap, but I was wrong about it hurting, I can still remember it twenty years on!

Knowing I was really lucky with the first birth, I didn't think I could possibly be that lucky second time around and when pregnant for the second time, I mentally prepared myself for a 'proper' labour. My waters broke at 6am. I rang the midwife, then got in the birthing pool, and told my husband to stop making the tea as he needed to deliver the baby.

This second labour lasted all of twenty minutes, and when the midwife arrived I was breastfeeding my new little boy. An hour later two more midwives turned up expecting to lend a hand, but they ended up with a glass of Champagne and a cuddle of the new baby.

Then came my third baby. I knew immediately this was a girl as it felt totally different to the other two pregnancies. And I was a moose, huge!

I was scared that after two text book pregnancies and two easy births, my luck couldn't possibly stretch to a third. I knew towards the end that I should stay at home as I might end up giving birth in the supermarket queue, but I had a business to run. I had a cleaning business, and along with my staff we cleaned around sixty houses a week, so I actually cleaned a house the day of the birth. I was short staffed and as it was my business, someone had to do it.

Fortunately my daughter didn't arrive until the evening. At 11pm, I turned the bedside light off, at 11.05 I turned it back on and rang the midwife. At 11.55 Millie arrived. As my births were always quick we decided not to bother with a pool this time and used the bath instead. So three babies with less than three hours in labour - probably a record. I wish it could be that easy for every woman.

After moving to Italy with my second husband and three children, I was unceremoniously dumped when he went back to the UK to his tart on the side, taking his wallet with him. But that's another story in another book.

I brought my kids up on my own in a country that has no child benefit system and no government handouts, with very little financial help from their father. We were desperately skint most of the time, but nobody died.

I have never been as poor as I have been in the last ten years but have never enjoyed life as much. I am in love with Italy; since moving here I have met the most amazing people, and have made some fantastic friends. I have three happy healthy kids who love and respect me, so all okay in the end. My two older children have left home to pursue their careers, so there's just me and my daughter in Italy now.

Now at forty-seven, my current mission in life is to find a normal man, if one exists - not married, not fat, and not a smoker, but they are a bit thin on the ground around here. Rural Italy has many attractions but Italian stallions are in short supply.

If one does not appear before my daughter flies the nest then I will sell my house and go travelling. Given that I am a hermit and get homesick at the end of my drive this idea actually horrifies me, so I think I may have to start taking the 'manhunt' a bit more seriously and find myself a husband.

I would rather work ten hours per week at a paid job and sit on a eighty-year-old sofa than work forty hours a week and then spend my weekend in Ikea choosing a chintzy lump of sponge to insult my lounge. My sofa was rescued from someone's garden fourteen years ago. I went to evening classes to learn how to upholster it and then I brought it to Italy. It's shabby as hell after three kids, five dogs and dozens of cats but I can and will revive it again - when I get a minute!

Restore, recycle and renovate is my hobby and my main job. I only work when I want to work. If I wake up and think, I can't be bothered today, I am going to stay home and cook/ dig the garden/go for a long walk, then that's what I will do. I don't have a materialistic bone in my body and have no need to earn loads to spend loads.

My various forms of employment involve the odd cleaning job here and there and property management - I look after seven houses for other ex-pats who use their houses for holiday homes or rental income. This keeps me busy in the summer months and keeps me and my daughter fed. In September when the work dries up I tend to panic a bit, but something always turns up.

I do renovating/decorating/repointing/plastering/tiling jobs for anyone who asks. I do airport taxi runs, in my bashed up half dead Fiat. I do cookery courses, teaching holidaymakers how to make fresh pasta, bread, ice cream and goats' cheese. I do internet marketing for a local estate agent and I also have a small income from a book I wrote about my life here in Italy. All of these things together mean I scrape through and manage to eat every day and pay the few bills I get and it works for me.

So many of my friends in the UK complain about their long hours and jobs that they hate, but they 'need' to have a new car every two years and to change their kitchen every five years. They 'need' a house with five toilets even though they only have three arses in residence.

This to me is totally baffling.

My house is tiny but in winter it is always toasty and warm, I don't worry about big fuel bills and I don't sit around in three jumpers. I am 'comfortable' and I love my life, I love my various jobs and enjoy the fact that I can do what I want when I want.

I am poor, like on a level that most people in the UK would consider six foot under the poverty line. My annual gross income is around five thousand Euros per year, but I eat good food and have a couple of glasses of wine every day. I have no credit cards, no loans and no savings. If my purse is empty then so is my fridge, but I can grow food, and I can source wood from my land to keep the house warm in winter.

I won't say I chose this lifestyle, because I didn't, it was forced on me by an ex-husband who did a runner and refused to support his family. But I have actually adjusted to it over the past ten years and found for me it is preferable to the overworked, stressed, materialistic lifestyle I see others not enjoying. My car doubles in value if I fill it with fuel and I can't close the driver's door as it won't open again if I do, but it gets me around and I won't bury it till it's definitely dead.

I have no desire to go on holiday as where I live is perfect. Although I have this silly notion that I am going to France for a few days this year!

After meeting two ladies on an authors' group online, we somehow became attached and ended up chatting every day. I now consider these two people to be really good friends even though we have never met ... yet.

Tottie (French Bird) - France

Apparently, I can start claiming my old age pension this year. There's clearly been some gross administrative cock-up as I can't possibly be that old. Mind you, I think my little house is haunted. Whenever I try to look in the mirror, I can't because there's this strange silver-haired woman with wrinkles who gets in front of me and I can only see her reflection.

I've been living in France for seven years now, in the wild and woolly Livradois-Forez region of the Auvergne. It's in the middle of France. If you stuck a pin into a map of France trying to hit the centre and I happened to be making one of my extremely rare visits to our principal city, Clermont-Ferrand, you would probably poke my eye out.

I moved to France in 2007 with my eighty-nine-year-old mother, who had dementia, and my manic depressive brother with a drink problem because, as they say, it seemed like a good idea at the time.

I spent four hard years as my mother's full-time carer,

dealing at the same time with my brother's mental health and drink-related issues, and working part-time as a freelance copywriter. When my mother died, after having a whale of a time living it up in France, I moved out to my own little retreat in the hills, affectionately known as Tottie's Grottage, as it was a very grotty cottage when I bought it. I live there quietly and eccentrically with my two border collies and two cats.

Eccentric, because the locals are convinced I am slightly mad. In no small measure, it's because I drive round in an old La Poste van covered in hippy stickers. There are poppies all over the bonnet and wings, flowers in abundance and lots of pagan symbols, like the Green Man and Kokopelli. Then there are the little sayings. They may be in English, but even the locals get the gist of statements like: 'Where have all the hippies gone?' on the back door.

I've been a writer most of my life. I originally trained and worked as a journalist, later retraining as a copywriter and copy editor, which is what I do and will continue to do part-time until I finally get some pension in my hot little hand. I write all sorts of stuff: press releases, catalogue copy, website pages and direct mailings. Ever thought what a lovely 'chap' the managing director of that firm is, who sends you all those warm and friendly personal letters and emails to let you know of the latest bargain offers? It's probably me who wrote them.

I now write books as well. I've written a trilogy of books about whatever possessed me to move to France as I did, how things worked out in France for my mother, and what I did with myself when she died, at the age of ninety-four, and I finally regained my freedom.

I've done all sorts of jobs to earn a crust – a small one, as I am not remotely materialistic and my tastes in life are simple. My idea of a designer label is Berghaus or Craghoppers. My jobs have included running my own holiday riding centre and managing a large commercial one for someone else, working in a further education college with horses to help young people with learning disabilities, and being an investigative journalist looking into the murky world of offshore finance and Ponzi schemes.

Though not lacking in ability, allegedly, I clearly had my ambition surgically removed at a very young age as I don't have any. I'm quite happy ticking along in my own sweet rhythm. As long as I can feed the animals and myself (note the order – it is significant) and go on some little camping trips to explore the countryside and wildlife of the region, that is more than sufficient for me.

I'm not remotely religious but I did once give up men for Lent and have so far never looked back. I was married, once, although I can't imagine why, and certainly not to the man I finished up with. I think I must have been drunk at the time.

He was an army officer, who rose to the rank of major, and the fairly brief time I spent living as a army wife in married quarters both in England and in Germany was possibly the most mind-numbingly boring period of my life. It was when I saw the brilliant Bryan Forbes film *The Stepford Wives* that I finally realised what was going on. The army wives I was trying to mix with weren't humanoid at all, they were robotic, devoid of a brain, entirely reprogrammed to support and pleasure their husbands and nothing more. This was confirmed to me when I was once forced to endure a wives only drinks party where those present spent much of their time discussing which NAAFI shop they preferred, based solely on the capacity of the shopping trolleys they provided. I only wish I could tell you that I was joking.

I always said in jest that I would break the monotony by having an affair with a black private soldier in the Pioneer Corps. That's because, me being an officer's wife, to associate with the dreaded 'other ranks' was too horrendous to contemplate for a 'wife of', as army wives were known everywhere. The Pioneer Corps were always considered the lowest of the low, being the gravediggers, not fit to lick the boots of the mighty Royal Artillery in which the Galloping Major served. And black because in those days it would be hard to imagine any body more institutionally racist than the army, in my experience. That was one of the things I found hardest to stomach, never having been remotely racist nor anything else -ist. In fact the one thing I find hard to tolerate is intolerance.

I did have the affair. I couldn't find a black Pioneer Corps private, unfortunately, but I do think my poker hand would have counted as a Royal Flush. How about white Rhodesian, Jewish, married, father of four, grandfather, ex-warrant officer, ex-mercenary, ex-Paras, ex-SAS, manager of the 'other ranks' NAAFI club?

The affair ended my marriage, of course, not that I regretted that. But if I'd always thought the expression 'broken heart' was a load of nonsense, it showed me that it wasn't. He absolutely broke my heart, beyond repair, and I've never loved anyone since.

It's been a long time since there's been a man in my life and that's fine, I can happily live without. Of course that makes many people convinced I'm a dyke. Their word, not mine. Unfortunately not. I say unfortunately as I've been lucky enough to have a woman fall seriously in love with me, someone who was quite prepared to up sticks and move with me to France in search of a new life. Though I loved her dearly as the closest of friends, that was all I could feel, so it was not to be and our paths sadly went in separate directions.

I never had any children, and never wanted any. There is not a maternal fibre of my being and I would have made a useless parent, not having had brilliant ones myself. I was always up front with my ex, long before we even thought of marriage, as I had always felt that way. Unsurprisingly, our divorce was acrimonious and the financial settlement in particular was bloody. One of the things that he threw at me was my refusal to give him children, as if it had come as some great shock and revelation to him. I dread to think what they would have turned out like if we had bred!

I have never been back to the UK since moving here, not even for a visit, and the very idea of it terrifies me now. I know I just could not cope. The crime rate here is so low I once not only left my van unlocked outside my local supermarket, I actually accidentally left it with the door wide open, and nothing was touched. I now hold dual French/British nationality, having been 'frogified', as I see myself here for the duration. I've even planted a young silver birch tree on my land, under which my ashes are to be scattered.

Not remotely a party animal, I don't go out a vast amount, although I'm a regular at my local library and all the little events in my adopted area. I have a small circle of close friends, both French and English, and we meet up, not often but often enough, to do coffee, or lunch, or afternoon tea. A lot of the pursuits I enjoy most are fairly solitary, like walking my dogs, watching wildlife, camping in weathers that only I could enjoy under canvas, gardening, and reading. A lot of my socialising these days is done via social media.

Which is how I came to meet up with the other two birds in this adventure – one in Italy, one in the UK.

# Chapter Three
# A Third Bird

**via email**

*Tottie: Hi Janet, how are you? Still building gorgeous walls? How's things with your book, any more developments?*

*My friend Jilli Pennington and I wondered if you might be interested in a 3-way writing project we have on the go which may make us a few bob. It would involve a very brief trip to Italy and then a road trip from there to me in France with Jilli, probably in late September, which you might not be up for.*

*We did have a third writer on board but her circumstances have changed and we don't want to let the idea sink as it could be a goer.*

*Anyway, just a thought. Would appreciate an early answer.*

*Thanks, and best wishes*
*Tots*

*Janet: Your idea sounds intriguing. Whilst I'm always up for adventure, I fear you may have misjudged my abilities. When we produced our book, Helen was the writer and she did ninety-nine per cent of the writing and was responsible for the layout of the story. I'm*

*always prepared to voice my opinion and can, of course, write, but I have to be honest and say I am not, in the sense of writing books, a writer.*
*My talent is definitely in putting together walls rather then words. Since you need a third writer, I would definitely be just a hanger-on and not a productive team member. Thanks for thinking of me though - I'm flattered that you did. If you ever have a wall building project.............!*

*Tottie: Writing ability is not a problem at all - I'm an editor, remember! What we need is a 'character', which is why we thought of you! Someone opinionated, not afraid to voice their views, and who would be available to come on this mad but brief trip. Oh, and I do have a seriously falling down wall in need of repair.*

*Janet: Well yes - definitely - I'm up for it. Count me in. I will need some notice as I need to make arrangements for my dogs and there's a small matter of a passport? Interested to hear more.*

*Tottie: Fantastic!!!!! How soon could you get a passport sorted?*
*The precept is very simple - 3 females who like to write, or talk about their lives, who might never have met up in real life (you and I missed one another by many years as I'd left the area) meet via social media and get along (I think we do?)*
*Then they decide to meet up to see if they hit it off in the flesh. Jilli is in Italy. The UK member of the triad flies out to Jilli's place, then those two do an epic road trip to meet up with me. I don't think the same idea has been done in such a way before.*

*What makes it different is we all write very candidly about how we feel about one another, both before, during and after the meet up. Hence we need very strong characters who aren't afraid to speak their minds rather than pussyfoot around.*
*You realise if we tell you all about our idea and you then back out we will have to come after you and hunt you down??*

*Jilli can tell you all about how to get to her. Would you be up for sharing the drive from there to here?*

*Janet: Driving - any distance - is no problem for me. I can drive anything anywhere!*

*Tottie: Fabulous, if you are on board, I think it would work!*

*Janet: Sounds good. I hope you realise you're inviting the mad axe-woman of Derbyshire to your homes!!! I'll have a look at what I need to do for a passport tonight - I'm currently sitting in a field with a wall. The idea sounds completely bonkers so I should fit in very well.*
*I'll let you know once I've looked into the passport website as to how long it takes to get one. I've really no idea.*

## Facebook – via Private Message

*Tottie: I've emailed Farmer Bird the outline and what we've put together so far so she can jump in and add her bits along the same lines.*

*Jilli: Fab! I have a good feeling about this. Looking*

*forward to seeing what she comes up with, and reading her feedback.*

**via email:**

*Jilli: Hi Janet, Tottie tells me you are in for the 3 birds book. We all need to get together at some point to have a 3 way chat. I believe you need a passport, that could be a problem as UK passport office is behind, Is there any chance you could go in person to the passport office with your forms (filled in) and photos/documents? That would ensure that you could get it quickly. Give it some thought, be sure it is for you and that you can commit to a week away and some time to get it all written up, and let us know.*

*Tottie: I think this could work really well but we all need to be committed to it and enthusiastic about it. I'm more than happy to do all the editing and licking stuff into shape, that's not a problem. What we want from each of us is complete candour and above all, if we hate one another on sight we need to be honest and say so. That's why I think this could work as I know none of us has a problem with that.*

*Janet: Absolutely. I'm fully committed (or should be!!) and have absolutely no problem with being forthright. I would certainly need help knocking anything I write into something usable. I'm NOT a natural writer. Provided you understand that - we're ok. I am reliable - if I say I'm going to do something I do it, so don't worry on that score.*

## later, by email:

*Janet: First thoughts on what I've read. I like what you've done so far. Bear in mind that chick lit and reading other people's messages to each other is one of my least favourite subjects (I'm very hard to please) but what you've set out did make me smile - so far so good. I love the new genre - chickality. That did make me laugh.*
*I think I need to be your watchdog on behalf of Possible Reader who isn't au fait (bit of badly spelt? French there for Tots) with modern digital terminology. I've no idea what PM is, unless its Pre-Menstrual.*

*Tottie: Getting a good feeling about this, Birds ;)*

*Janet: Try HRT.*

\* \* \*

Janet (Farmer Bird) – England

*dictated, via voice-recorder*

I'm Janet, a sixty-four-year-old retired farmer and still working drystone waller, from the Peak District, Derbyshire. Inevitably, the other two call me Farmer Bird, as for forty years I farmed a small hill farm, keeping eighty head of beef cattle, horses and poultry, and doing it on my own for all but six of those years.

I grew up in New Mills, where I had a very happy childhood, brilliant parents. My mum and dad were both lovely people, and I got along with my brother ok. My half brother, if we're being correct (*Oh God, now the dog's trying to lick me because I'm talking to no one*) although we were never terribly close because he was eleven years older than me.

I had a lovely time as a child, going out to play every day. Of course there were no computers, no mobile phones, no Facebook, just playing outside, sledging in the winter with all my friends. In the summer months, outside school hours, there would be about eight of us, all around ten or eleven years old, who would play together daily.

I had two close friends, Pat and Joyce, and one day we were playing in an old quarry, very near to our houses, where we had built a camp on a rocky ledge. You had to climb about eight feet up a rock face to get to the camp (quite a big climb for ten-year-olds) and, naturally, our respective parents had forbidden us to climb up there, which immediately added to the attraction.

On this particular day the three of us were in our camp when Pat inadvertently stepped off the edge and plunged onto the floor beneath. Joyce and I scrambled down, already starting to cry as Pat lay unmoving on the ground. She had hit her head on a stone and there was a tiny trickle of blood running from her forehead. We poked her tentatively but there was no response. I seem to recall that our main concern at the time was that we would be in trouble for climbing the rocks – not that Pat was in need of some attention.

We ran to our respective homes and I stood in our kitchen washing my hands and sniffling. "Dinner's ready, sit at the table", said Mum. I sat down staring at the tablecloth. Dad put down his paper and sat at the table. "What've you been up to this morning?".

"Nothing much," I responded as the first tear rolled down my cheek. Mum put our plates on the table, then stared at me and said: "What on earth's wrong, Janet. What's happened?" "Pat's dead!" I wailed. There followed a moment's silence, then: "What? What on earth are you talking about?" The tears were flowing freely now but I managed to explain that Pat had 'fallen over' in the quarry and that she was lying on the floor and was therefore dead. "Right" said Dad, standing up, "Janet, take us to where Pat's fallen". We ran round to the quarry where we found Joyce's parents with Pat, who was sitting up groggily by now. An ambulance was summoned via the phone box at the corner of the road (no mobiles in those days and very few houses had their own phones). Pat was taken to hospital and released later that day with a minor bump on her head. We never did admit that she'd fallen off the ledge.

Not long after this we had our own telephone installed in the hallway at home. It was very exciting. We were on a party line, which was common in the late nineteen-fifties, and if you picked up the handset and someone was already on the party line you could listen in to their conversation and join in if you wanted. You couldn't use your phone to make your own call until the other person had finished.

Our phone was in the hall, next to the front door. Since we did not have any form of heating in the house other than coal fires in the living room and front room, there was no danger of spending my dad's money by making long calls to friends because for much of the year the temperature in the hall was little more than freezing!

We used to go on holiday every year. My parents weren't wealthy people but they weren't poor either. We often went to the Isle of Man, which was my dad's favourite, although my mum was always sick as we used to go by ship. On one memorable occasion she vomited her false teeth over the rail of the ship and lost them. She spent the next two weeks having a holiday in the Isle of Man with no teeth in, which I found hilarious.

If we didn't go to the Isle of Man, we went to Blackpool. Of course we didn't have a car and we used to think we were going such a long way, although it was only about sixty-five miles. I loved my holidays, we had such good times.

Then in the sixties my dad got his first car which caused great excitement as not many people in our neighbourhood at that time had family cars. It was a Ford Prefect and it used to stay in the garage all week. My dad would take it out every day and polish it then put it back in the garage. Then on a Sunday we'd all go out for a drive, which was great fun.

I like to tell stories from the past as well, as my life has been full of amusing incidents, like the infamous day I managed to wreak havoc armed only with a pre-war potato harvester and two nervous Shire horses. Then there was the early notoriety when one of my bullocks escaped and went galloping down Glossop High Street with me, the police and local newspaper reporters running behind.

Friends often comment that I like to tell a lot of jokes. It's true, I do like a laugh, but it's sometimes also a way of skating over things I prefer not to talk about. I actually started out to write a book based on the amusing experiences in my life but soon found they were overshadowed by other memories which were not so funny. It's all told in my book so I won't repeat it here, except to say that not all of my notoriety has been as funny as escaping bullocks or stampeding Shires.

I've chosen to live in a caravan as my needs are very simple and I like the freedom I have to move around anywhere and any time I want. I'm lucky to be based at a friend's farm in the Derbyshire Dales on a site which is not only very quiet and secluded but also very scenic.

Like most farmers, holidays were seldom on the agenda in my adult life, although I did once visit Switzerland on a school trip in the 1960s. I loved it! After the family holidays in either Blackpool or the Isle of Man, it was really exciting at that time to go abroad. We went by coach and stayed in Lucerne next to Lake Lucerne. Our hotel had bedrooms with balconies which were actually over the Lake itself. For a few of my teenage years I had episodes of sleepwalking, which were getting less and less frequent, but I was a bit nervous in case I should sleepwalk and fall over the balcony into the lake. I couldn't swim! One of my lasting memories of the trip was my friend

Jennifer, who I shared the room with, making me close my eyes whilst she surreptitiously locked the balcony doors and hid the key!

I remember visiting Hergiswil and the Eiger, and going in a cable car, which was a real adventure. We went on Lake Lucerne in a little motor boat for two. I was reluctantly paired off with a baker's son who was extremely fat, spotty and sweaty and I pushed him overboard when he tried to put his arm round me. It didn't occur to me to wonder if he could swim! He could and was rescued in minutes by a supervising boat, but, of course, we were both in trouble for 'fooling round'.

I didn't actively dislike school but I did struggle at secondary school from the beginning because I was put in a class where the pupils had already done a term and I was expected to just catch up. I was always bottom of every class until I got to fifteen, then I had three new teachers who actually taught and explained things properly and I improved so much that by the time I took CSE (Certificate of Secondary Education) exams I did well and was offered a place at Grammar School to take GCE (General Certificate of Education) A levels (Advanced).

Because animals have long been my passion I always wanted to be a vet. But when the opportunity to go to grammar school arose, I already had my first job. My dad pointed out that I would have to take science, a subject girls didn't usually take at secondary school in those days. He was worried I would really struggle to get university grades and I think he was probably right. In the end I turned down grammar school and continued working.

My first job when I left school was as a trainee comptometer operator at the local Calico Printers' Association engraving works. I expected to hate it but I actually loved it. Small office, nice people, and a high salary – four pounds ten shillings a week! I felt like I was rolling in money. One of the cashiers earned ten pounds a week and I tried to imagine ever earning so much! The CPA closed its works four years later and I was made redundant. I then went to work at a local solicitors' office as a trainee probate clerk.

I have no children. Apart from a few odd years in the late 70s when I went a bit broody I've never really wanted any. My three dogs - a Staffordshire Bull terrier and two Jack Russells - keep me company for many hours whilst I'm walling and, although they are all in their teenage years, I'm hopeful they'll be around for many years to come.

I have some great-nieces but I'm not in contact with them. I've never been very close to my half brother, because of the eleven year age gap. My mum married his dad who was then killed in the Second World War whilst my mum was pregnant. Mum remarried a few years later and then I was born. My brother was dating and getting married when I was still about ten so we always had different lives.

Since then I think my lifestyle, criminal charges and a prison sentence (all revealed in my book) have clearly been an embarrassment to him and I now have no contact with him or his family. He has two daughters who in turn have children of their own.

I sold my farm some time ago and now live quietly in a caravan in a beautiful village in the Derbyshire Dales. I spend my days drystone walling and looking after my three terriers. I've been a drystone waller for fifty years and these days I find the work very relaxing and fulfilling. I can work on my own in isolated areas, which I prefer, and can also earn a little extra spending money which helps my pension stretch further.

Walls don't just have ears, they often have a tale to tell. I sometimes find items left in them from over a hundred years ago - particularly bottles - and I find it fascinating to think that the walls I build today may well be here in a hundred years or more, although I doubt I'll be around to check!

As well as walling and walking the dogs I also enjoy cycling (in nice weather of course) and love playing

Badminton which I do several times a week.

I've never been on a plane and suddenly I'm caught up in this idea and planning to fly off to countries I've never been to, to meet up with two people I've only ever chatted to via Facebook and email, who seem to be best friends already. Luckily they both seem to be about as mad as I am, so I'm hoping we will all get on.

**via email:**

> *Janet: Right, I've been on the passport website. The bad news is I can't apply in person at the passport office - that service is not currently available unless they ask you to attend. The quickest way I can apply is online and the time given for issue is 6 weeks. Since I will need a passport sometime in the future I've filled in the forms, paid the fee and applied online. Estimated date of issue is 22nd September.*
> *I know you'd probably not expected this problem and if you'd rather not wait please go ahead with someone else - I won't hold it against you and I can't come over and beat you up as I've no passport!!!!*
> *Over to you.*
>
> *Tottie: Hey, you don't get out of it that easily. You are the chosen one, there is no escape!*
>
> *Janet: HA! It's all systems go then. Will I need any vaccinations? I assume not for Italy and France but best to check. You and Jilli don't have any contagious diseases I hope?*
>
> *Tottie: We both have rabies but are under court orders to wear muzzles at all times in public. No, you are fine in both countries but you need to get yourself*

*an EHIC, a European Health Insurance Card, so you are covered just in case.*

*Janet: Thanks - will do. Rabies is no problem - I've had it. It made me very thirsty!*

*Tottie: LOL! It's your sense of humour that got you hired for this job.*

**later, by email**

*Tottie: Hi Janet, Thanks for throwing yourself right into this project with such enthusiasm!*
*I have an idea. We know you can tell a very good tale but as you say, writing it down doesn't come as easily. Would you use a dictaphone? Perhaps ramble into that then let me type it all up and edit as I go? We could sort you out with one soonish to get you started, then you could bring it out with you for the road trip and your reflections afterwards, then send me the tapes or whatever the thing has. Techie I am not!.*
*What do you think?*

*Janet: That sounds like a really good idea - I have no problem at all with talking!!! If it's not too much trouble for you I think it would probably work better. Thanks.*

*Tottie: No problems at all! I will source one and arrange to get it delivered to you then we can really crack on.*

*Jilli: Well I was thinking at some point of making a Facebook page for the book and posting video footage of the road trip, and photos of our meetings etc, maybe start it before we kick off proper but keep it private so nobody can see it until we are ready. Thoughts, Birds?*

*Tottie: All very positive, going in the right direction. Next step is to source a decent dictaphone which I will try to do in the next day or two.*

**later, via email**

*Tottie: Well that's a morning of my life I'll never get back! Who'd'a thought choosing a voice recorder would be so mind-boggling??*

*Janet, without wishing to give offence, I've gone on the assumption that you're as much of a technophobe as I am so have chosen one which is as simple as possible, voice activated, doesn't connect to a PC or anything, you just talk, record and playback.*
*It should be with you next week sometime and I'm hoping delivery is no problem - I forgot in your funny country you don't have secure letter boxes the posties have keys for like they do here, so hope it will arrive and will do the job.*
*It was only 30 quid, we can claw it back from our first book sales!*

*Janet: Thanks Tots - none taken! You're quite right to go for simple. I've only just stopped using a quill!!! I note you're expecting to sell £30 worth of books. There's optimism for you.*

*Tottie: Stick with us, Farmer Bird, we'll make you rich!*

# Chapter Four
# All of a Twitter

Jilli

I first got into social media in a big way as it was a great way to market my book all over the world. Though when I started out on Facebook and Twitter I had a PC and managed to do it quite easily, I now have a Mac and am struggling to 'friend' it. I am not computer savvy and absolutely hate the Mac.

I know I am in the minority but if I had money I would go out and buy a PC (proper computer) and bin the Mac at the first opportunity. I know it is not the laptop's fault, I am completely to blame, but if it isn't easy I am not interested, I read books not instruction manuals. PCs are easy, Macs aren't. But I have learnt as much (and only as much) as I need or think I need to know, to get by.

At first I figured, living abroad, that social media would be useful for keeping up with family and friends in the UK. Turned out most of the people I wanted to keep up with didn't do social media! So I made new friends, and then rediscovered old friends, people I hadn't seen or spoken to for ten or fifteen years.

I found people from school - although I only went once they remembered me! - and I hooked up with so many people. It was fantastic to catch up with them, find out who they married and how many kids they ended up with.

# ALL OF A TWITTER

I love social media, it is great for old friends and new. I have sold books all over the world, thanks to Facebook and Twitter. It's a very useful tool if you know how to use it and I use it a lot. I have a television but rarely switch it on, because I would rather spend my evenings catching up with people.

It can have a downside though. I write, usually about my life, and I share everything, hold nothing back. I do sometimes get myself into trouble for saying too much and this can attract the wrong kind of attention. I get my fair share of weirdos. To date I have had four stalkers, one of whom was a woman. I got rid of her twice, but she kept coming back with a new name. There are some very strange people on the internet, and a lot of crazy behaviour but it's free entertainment, and there is a delete/block button for when it stops being funny.

There is so much help and advice out there though. If anybody has a question or a problem they can put it out and have it solved within the hour. Why would anyone not want to take advantage of so much information? I have friends who refuse to join in, which reminds me of my mum saying "why would anyone want a mobile phone?" Unfortunately, if you try to fight progress you will get left behind, so I do my best to keep up. I seem to be jogging along behind everyone else, but having a teenager in residence certainly helps when it gets really tricky.

Whilst trying to find ways to market my book, I joined a number of book/writer groups which is where I first met Tottie Limejuice. She, like me, had left 'Shitey Blighty' for a better place, and had written about her experiences. Hers was a different story and a different country (France) but we had so much in common and seemed to be very similar in the wit and sarcasm area.

We got on really well and chatted, swapped stories, shared ideas and advice. She also introduced me to her friend Janet and the three of just seemed to be on the same planet. One of these days we are going to be in the same country!

# TAKE THREE BIRDS

Tottie

So what is this social media stuff then? My friend and work colleague in England, Sarah, who sends me enough copywriting work to keep the wolf from the door, mentioned that a lot of our clients wanted to establish a social media presence. One of our largest clients in particular wanted to be on Twitter and to post lots of tweets, which I was going to be writing for them.

Fab. Cool. Right on. I made suitably knowing noises in advertising-speak via email to my friend but in truth I hadn't a clue what any of it meant. Never heard of Twitter, the only tweets I knew of came from the birds in my garden, tuning up for the dawn chorus.

I daily worship at the feet of whoever invented Google, and this was no exception. I soon learned enough to set myself up with a Twitter account and start making tentative attempts at these new-fangled tweets.

Dogs are a bit passion of mine. I've had dogs for more than forty years, could never see myself being without one, so I started off by making contact with other dog-lovers and was soon chatting to a nice bunch of people. Well they were bound to be. Dog people are usually, though not invariably, very nice.

What a bunch of bores I had come across in my army wife days. One pompous colonel, knowing my love of dogs, and that I owned an adored German Shepherd Dog, attempted to strike up conversation with me at a dinner night by beginning: "I don't like dogs", as if it were something to be proud of. My response of: "I generally find I don't like people who don't like dogs', didn't go down too well."

Through dogs, I got chatting to more and more people, with wider interests. Social media, I discovered, was just like having the pen-pals I had had when I was at school, though, in the case of Twitter, with fewer words. The strict one hundred and forty character limit on Twitter didn't bother me unduly –

copywriters often have to write to a very rigid word count to fit allocated space.

When I was younger I'd written to pen-pals in France, Africa and Malaysia. We'd exchanged news of what we'd been doing all day, what we did at the weekend and what things were like at school in our different countries. Twitter was a bit like that, it seemed, only more spontaneous.

Chatting to some of the bright young things on social media made me feel younger. But then I have always had trouble with the dreaded 'act your age'. Nobody ever issued me with a handbook to tell me how to start being an old wrinkly of sixty-plus. So I enjoyed hanging out with a younger crowd online and feeling thirty once more.

I'd made early forays into the mysterious world of Facebook, which I quickly labelled 'The Dark Side' as I could not fathom my way round it at all to begin with. Gradually I found many of its features to be much better than Twitter's, particularly the ease of chatting to several people at once without taking up most of your permitted Twitter word count with 'tagging' people into a conversation.

Because I write books, I started joining various book groups on the internet, which is where I met Jilli, or Doris, as I quickly started calling her. It was also on one of these that I came across Janet and read her book, which I found a rattling good read, like a well-paced crime thriller, only true.

We became cyber-friends on the writers' site, supporting one another's books and chatting both on the forum and via email. I introduced Janet to Jilli. We all read and reviewed one another's books and seemed to develop a strong mutual respect. Mind you, I gave Jilli's book five stars, and she only gave mine four stars, but I've learned to forgive her.

So suddenly here we were. Three birds who have never met, in three different countries. Different backgrounds, some similar interests, some light years apart. Jilli and her non-stop necking of the wine? Well, back in my misspent youth I was the same, or worse, but sadly no more. Janet and her badminton? I've always loathed sport in any form, either as a competitor or spectator, except show jumping which I used to do a lot. I only ever took up the violin at school because it got me out of hated lacrosse practice.

Now our daily rituals were expanding to include long, hilarious and sometimes smutty emails and private messages on Facebook which would have the three of us laughing till the tears ran down our legs in our separate countries.

So then Doris hatched the plot that we should all give it a go at meeting up in one country – France, since, like a good wine, I don't travel, and it was geographically in the middle.

We must be mad!

Janet

What do I think of social media? Ha! Don't really like it, never have. I've tried my best to use it and sometimes enjoy doing so but overall I think my view of things like Facebook (I've never mastered Twitter) is that I find it intensely irritating to spend so much time on a site like that just talking what seems to me to be drivel.

People appear to be posting pictures of themselves, and pictures of their friends and saying what they did today, and a lot of the time they are conversing with people they see regularly. I like silence. I can talk, for England - if you get me going on a subject that interests me I can gabble on with the best of people - but I also like to spend a lot of time being quiet.

However I do see social media's good side. I think for anyone who's housebound for whatever reason it must be an absolute boon to be able to use social networking sites to talk to people at very low cost or no cost at all. And if you have friends and family abroad, places you can't get to, it's a wonderful thing to be able to keep in touch through such sites, talk to them as if they were in front of you.

Once I'm on there, I can join in and talk, and I have used it for book marketing to good effect. I even did a course about using social media. I was astonished to hear that you should be posting at least eight or ten times a day – the more the better. I questioned the figures as I had visions of being sat on Facebook all day!

I did start posting a bit about my ambition to walk the Appalachian Trail, across the USA, and I thought well, at least I am learning something myself while I'm doing it. But generally I found it a bit of an effort and I'd rather not go on my laptop at all, unless I've got some work to do as I had to do when Helen Parker and I published our book.

I needed to become familiar with Amazon, with publishing an ebook and with marketing it via Facebook, Twitter and other sites. Helen took on Twitter and I deal with our Facebook page. I post regularly and do what I have to since there's little point in publishing a book but not marketing it. However, I restrict it to evenings since I much prefer to be outside walling or doing something else outside in the daytime. I can easily live without social media!

**via email:**

*Janet: Recorder safely received. This is a simple one ? OMG!*

*Tottie: Oh dear! hope you manage.*

*Janet: Well, I've got the batteries in!*

*Tottie: Well done! That's quicker than I would have managed it.*

## later, via email

*Tottie: How are you getting on? Managed to switch it on yet?*

*Janet: Hi. Yes, I can now switch it on, put the batteries in and even take them out again!!! I think I've mastered it now - so time to start talking. Presumably if I cover my views on social media and what I think of you both so far - having never met you or spoken to you - that will be it until I get out there ?*
*No sign of passport yet but I've got everything else sorted.*
*I hope you both know I've never flown before! I've been looking at the restrictions - OMG. If I can pass through Manchester and Bologna airports without a problem and without getting lost it'll be a miracle. I can just feel your confidence in me growing!*

*Tottie: Wow, fabulous!!!! A first-time flyer! I hate it, but don't let that put you off, you may absolutely love it!*

## via Facebook Private Message

*Tottie: Wow! Amazing! Farmer Bird is a virgin flyer!*

*Jilli: She only flies with Virgin??*

*Tottie: No, you Doris, an actual virgin flyer as in, she has never flown. Sixty-four and has only been abroad once, to Switzerland, by coach, on a school trip years ago. Really brave lady, what an adventure, to fly out here, first time on a plane, and come and join up with a pair of nutters like us!*

## later, via email

*Janet: It's just occurred to me that I've been assuming that I will be staying with both Jilli and Tottie in your homes! It also occurs to me that that is a very rude presumption. Sorry. It naturally does not follow that I will be staying with you and maybe I need to be checking out relevant places to stay. Can you give me some pointers to local 'staying' places - perhaps the equivalent of B & B or camping sites near to you. Remember - as a person who lives in a field, I have very high standards!!!*

*Tottie: Don't be daft, 'course you will be staying with us! First night at Jilli's place in Italy, possibly in her fabulous Goat Cottage, then with me in my grottage (or in my tent if you prefer!) and I will do my best to ensure my dog Ci doesn't bite you - well, not too often at least. Then back to Jilli's for another night before departure.*

*Jilli: Well at my place you have options, my spare room - single bed in the office - or you can have Goat Cottage, which is a converted goat shed in the middle of a field. I think this will be home from home to you. Have a look at the video on the Goat Cottage Page on Facebook.*

*Tottie: Chez moi there's the spare room or the big tent for either/both of you.*

*Janet: Thank you both very much, that's very kind of you. I don't think I can stay in Goat Cottage as I've been baaahed. Seriously, Jilli, I'm more than happy to stay in your spare room - whichever is easiest for you.*

*I've received my Health Card this morning. So I'm all ready when the passport arrives. Getting excited now. Dogs trying to make me feel guilty!*

*Tottie. Whoot-whoot, this is going to be brilliant!! I certainly won't charge B&B as you have the air fare to find. Can't speak for Doris though - she is a Tyke, after all.*

*Janet: Staying with a Tyke? She should pay me!*

*Jilli: Noo, absolutely not, if we pool our resources we can do it without spending too much. I am happy to muck in with cooking/cleaning at yours when we get there to pay my way, and sort out any odd jobs you need doing when we aren't touring the soap shop etc.*

*Janet: Ohhhhh - are we going to a soap shop? This gets better and better!*

*Tottie: Yes, there is the most fab artisan soap place just near me and their stuff is addictive - and very reasonable!*

*Janet: Never use the stuff - except on Christmas day! Oh and I sometimes shower on my birthday!*

*Tottie: You'll fit right in here, then.*

*Jilli: By the way, I need a nice photo of you both, smiling happy type shot, to make a FB page about the book.*

*Janet: Here's one - me in front of one of my walls. Is this good enough? If you need better quality I'll have to take one with my camera.*

*Jilli: A bit wishy-washy but I found a good one on your own page, of you in the caravan. If it's ok to use it, I will.*

*Janet: Yes, go for it. Don't remember that one - I'm not in the nude I hope! That'll be no way to encourage Likes!!!*

*Jilli: Excellent, made me giggle - love your sense of humour! Tottie, I got the nice one of you and the lavender if it's ok to use that one?*

*Tottie: Lilac, Doris. And yes, that's fine*

*Jilli: Ok I have a photo of you both..pending approval. Now I want to know what bird you want as your own symbol. I am having the heron cos it's my favourite thing in the world. See, now you know something else about me! So pick a bird, Birds!*

*Tottie: Mine's the short-toed eagle.*

*Janet: A turkey.*

*Jilli: Oh you are hilarious woman, we are gonna have a scream!*

*Janet: Jilli says we're gonna have ice cream. Strawberry for me with sprinkles.*

*Tottie: Oh no, don't get me started on Morgan Freeman and titty sprinkles.*

## TAKE THREE BIRDS

*Janet: I do hope we're not going to be subjected to filthy pornography on this holiday. Disgusted of Derbyshire. (And do we have to pay extra for it?)*

*Tottie: No, only clean pornography here, we do use soap ;)*

*Jilli: Holiday? Holiday? Oh dear no, it is no holiday.*

# Chapter Five
# Bird Watching

Jilli

They say that Facebook friends aren't real, but when you really click with someone and end up chatting every day, whether you have met in person or not doesn't matter, they become important. That's how it was for me and Tottie.

When she went off the radar for three days, I noticed within a matter of hours. Us writers spend a lot of time online, so four hours of nothing is a long absence and I started wondering. Then after a whole day without contact, me and a few others started worrying.

Not worrying in the 'little old lady who lives alone' sense because Tottie is far from 'biddyhood'. She is a very young sixty-something, very independent, capable, strong and resourceful – she goes camping in the snow for gawd's sake (nutjob). But anyone of any age who lives alone should have regular contact with others just in case of accident.

I decided to check up on her and see what was going on. Through Facebook I traced her brother who I knew lived in France and although not close by, he may be able to contact her by phone and check up on her. I sent him a message and waited. Ten minutes later when I had heard nothing I went looking for other people who were living in the same area. I found one of her friends and messaged her.

By the end of the day both had replied, and they told me a snow storm had taken out all the power, so that Tottie had no phone/internet or mobile signal and was completely out of reach. But she was ok and would be back online as soon as she could.

I think it was around this point I figured out how strong our friendship had become, because I was genuinely worried and missed our daily chats.

Tottie gives the impression of having had a very interesting life so far, lots of things keep spilling out in conversation that shock and surprise me. Our chats are always entertaining and we have a real giggle. A similar sense of humour and sarcastic licence mean we are often in tune and end up typing the same or similar remarks.

She comes across as well educated, with common sense, a mind always open and happy to take on board new things and ideas, which is why I knew she would get involved in this project and start throwing in new ideas to get the ball rolling.

I have read all her books but still feel like there is a lot more to her and can't wait to hear about it.

I think she is a very honest, straight laced person, who tells it like it is but does so in a tactful way so will never openly upset or offend.

Like when she read my book for instance. It desperately needed a 'proper edit' so she took it and tidied it up, taking the piss at regular intervals as she went through it, but never criticizing. As a writer it's always good to have a friend like this.

Tottie

Call a spade a spade? Jilli calls a spade a bloody shovel! Downright down to earth, what you see is what you get, strongly self-opinionated, (and why not?) and with an opinion on just about everything.

Younger than I am, older than some of my new circle of online friends, although I could still just about have been her mother. Once Jilli and I in particular got chatting together, out of sight of the public, forget thirty-something – we quickly regressed to our teens. We shared a very similar sense of humour and also a sense of fair play. We were always ready to sweep in and fight the corner of the underdog if we sensed any injustice.

Jilli's life had been tough. She'd been scarily short of money at times but with her natural resourcefulness, had always managed to pull through each crisis. I could relate to that. Been there, done that, got the T-shirt. I liked and admired the way she didn't whinge about it, just got on with it.

I also hugely admired her single-minded drive in marketing her book, and felt I could learn a lot from her on that score. It didn't win her a lot of friends in some of the book groups, where she was sometimes talked about as 'too pushy', usually by people who sold far fewer books than she did, of course.

But there was also a very strongly compassionate side to her nature which shone through, sometimes despite herself. Her readiness to take in stray animals was a bit of a giveaway.

Jilli was a Yorkshire lass, a Tyke, as people from that county are known, and it's not an area known for its tact and diplomacy. Our Doris, as I often called her, had not yet learned that sometimes, no matter how strongly you feel about something, it's best just to bite your tongue until it bleeds and say nowt, as us folk from 'oop north' say.

With the benefit of my extra years and more miles on the clock, I was learning a bit more control, although not total. People often misjudged us both, convinced they knew our motives when they clearly didn't, so our ability to offend unintentionally simply by speaking our minds was another factor in common.

I also discovered Jilli was a good friend, and a loyal one, who had my back. When abnormally early and very heavy snowfall on trees still in full leaf knocked out power and telephone lines around my little 'grottage' and I was missing from social media, it was Doris who noticed first and took action.

With great initiative, she found my brother's contact details through Facebook to find out if I was all right. Mobile phone signals are very poor here at the best of times, especially when blocked by heavy snow and low cloud, but I had managed to get one text off to him to tell him what had happened. Once Jilli knew, she let cyberspace know through my own Facebook page.

It's a reflection of the times and a measure of how much time many of us now spend on social media that she noticed my absence so quickly!

We got on very well with nearly eight hundred kilometres separating us. It never occurred to me that we might meet up, since I almost never leave my beloved Auvergne and although I'd told Jilli she was always welcome here, I knew her financial situation made it very unlikely she would ever travel this far.

Back in the UK, our paths would most probably never have crossed. Our backgrounds were completely different, our interests in that past life divergent. Books were what initially brought us together, both being self-published writers of our experiences of making a new life in a new country.

We went on to form a Facebook Book Group between us, with another friend, Posh Bird, which gives us a lot of fun and has widened our circle of friends. We have occasional guest spots on it, and one of our early guests was Farmer Bird Janet, together with her co-writer Helen Parker, and brilliant guests they both turned out to be.

It's one thing to meet, chat and become friends on social media. It's another thing entirely to meet up in the flesh and expect the friendship to be the same.

Were we completely insane even to contemplate it?

Time would tell!

Jilli

I met Janet through Tottie, and discovered we were all in the same writers' group. So we had the chance to read each others work before we published.

Janet has certainly had a very interesting past, and her book is quite a shocker; but besides 'that story' her life has been fascinating. With a passion for farming from a very young age, she knew that she wanted to work with animals and was determined to get there in the end. A real grafter, working long hours, doing the kind of work that some men would find hard going, Janet seemed to just get on with it and really love it.

She still enjoys the outdoor lifestyle, living on a farm and spending her time building dry stone walls to earn a living, despite being in her early sixties. How do I keep finding these older ladies who refuse to embrace 'biddyhood'? Aren't they supposed to take up knitting and start peeing their pants somewhere between sixty and seventy? I really hope I am like these birds when I grow up.

First impression of Farmer Bird was maybe she was a bit of a hermit/recluse who preferred being alone, enjoying peace and quiet, as she lives in a caravan with only her dogs for company. Then I started email correspondence with her and my daughter kept wondering why I had tears rolling down my face. Within minutes of opening her messages I would be howling with laughter. The woman is a nutter, hilarious doesn't cover it, that sense of humour should be bottled and sold on the open market. I am so looking forward to meeting her because I think it's going to be non-stop laughter from day one.

I do feel though, that behind this entertaining, lively lady there is a lot of sadness carried from her past and whilst she has written about it in her book, and speaks openly about it, there must be scars that will never heal. For someone to come out the other side retaining the ability to laugh as she has done is something of an achievement, when there are still so many unanswered questions.

So she has agreed to join our triangle, has been interviewed by the passport office, managed to book her first ever flight online, got all her documents and sorted a puppy-sitter. All she has to do now is find Manchester airport, sit back and enjoy the flight.

Then the madness begins and I can't wait. I must now blow the dust off the corkscrew ready for her arrival.

Tottie

Crime thrillers are my favourite read. Although I write what could loosely be described as travel memoirs, it's always to the crime section of the library I head first. I'm an enthusiastic member of my local library in France and enjoy the annual reading circle of crime novels.

Through a writers' site on the internet, I discovered Janet's book and was in my element. In parts it read like a really good police thriller, with a couple of unexpected twists which had me glued to my computer screen reading when I should have been doing other things.

As a bonus, it was a true story, and I'd even read some parts of it in the newspapers, since Janet and I had grown up barely ten miles apart, though our paths had never crossed.

For me, there were a couple of police procedural issues which niggled. One in particular was one of those 'but if they'd done that, surely they'd have known about that' scenarios.

The particular site on which I first met Janet made it very easy to contact writers with observations so I contacted her and asked her the questions which were bothering my little brain. I quickly discovered her to be a very direct and open person; her response was swift, candid and made total sense.

We became friends on the site, frequently chatting on various forum topics. Her humour was quick-fire and quick-witted, her sense of irony perfectly matched my own and she could certainly pun for Britain.

I formed the opinion from the outset that had we ever met in real life, we could have been friends, probably because of rather than despite her somewhat chequered recent past. I've always had great admiration for someone who acts boldly, outrageously even, then has the nerve to admit their actions and take the consequences.

It's just possible that our paths had in fact crossed in our earlier lives without either of us knowing or recollecting. Both pony mad, we discovered later that we had competed in the same gymkhanas. We'd possibly even gone head to head in the odd bending race, or battled it out for a pole in the musical hats.

As well as chatting on the author site, we took to exchanging emails, having a general chat, touching base. Penpals, of the electronic kind.

Janet is now also someone I've come to count as a friend without ever thinking we would meet. Yet she will shortly be making an amazingly long and convoluted journey to visit me.

Hopefully, being a bit older, she may exert some sort of a good influence on Doris and they will both arrive here safely. I am known for being an eternal optimist!

Janet

I first met both Tottie and Jilli on an authors' website called Authonomy where we had our books posted and we had to comment on each others' books. I read Tottie's book first and then Jilli's. When I read Tottie's book and commented on it, she did the same with our book. She then contacted me because she had some questions about our book. She was very forthright; she asked what she wanted to know and I answered the questions and we began conversing in that way.

I was then astonished to find out that she was a similar age to me and that she had grown up just a few miles from where I lived. We'd never met but we seemed to have similar interests, in some ways very similar sort of lives, when we were younger, in particular a love of horses and riding.

As a teenager I used to go to Pony Club rallies every week with my pony, Lucky. These were usually held at Offerton, Cheshire, which is the area where Tottie lived and I also went to many shows and gymkhanas in that area. Since Tottie was also a keen rider we may well have met on many occasions in the past, little knowing our paths would cross all these years later.

We seem to have a great deal in common. A love of horses, dogs and all of nature, the outdoor life and living simply. Over a period of a few months I gained the impression that Tottie was not just an intelligent person because of the jobs she'd held and the things she'd done but a strong personality, forthright in the way she spoke and with a very good sense of humour. As I read Tottie's trilogy of books about her move to France and her immediate family, my view of her as a person who takes life on and gets things done was strengthened. I also realised there was no mention at all of boyfriends, a partner, a husband, children etc and so I assumed that she had remained single.

But then I also feel that there is much more to Tottie and a great deal yet to learn.

\* \* \*

From reading Jilli's book I was left with the impression of a very direct Yorkshire woman, with drive and energy, but one who had been dealt some poor cards, leaving her, a few years ago, in a foreign country with little money and three young children. Someone who I think is resourceful and determined. I remember reading some of her comments on other people's books on Authonomy. I recall one book which was, in my humble opinion, very poorly written. The grammar, punctuation and spelling were quite appalling and the story was non-existent. I always found it hard to comment on such books as I felt I should find at least one positive thing to say and I really couldn't in this case. I chickened out by simply highlighting all the spelling and punctuation errors in the first chapter. I then read Jilli's review and had to smile at its directness. She had clearly spent time on reading the book and on writing her review. She packed a full punch first of all by listing all the faults of the writing (which were many) but then, rather than leaving it at that, she offered the author some excellent down to earth advice and offered to help in any way she could if the author needed some assistance.

That, for me, summed Jilli up. Very direct and blunt – to the point of being in your face with her opinion – but underneath that a kind, warm and very genuine person. I also feel that underneath the bluff exterior there may be a touch of vulnerability which in turn may come from the difficult years she's had in the past.

**via email**

> *Jilli: By the way Farmer Bird, with you not having ever been further afield than Bridlington, just wondered if you are aware that we foreigners drive on the wrong side of the road, and our steering wheel is in the passenger seat?*
>
> *Tottie: But don't worry about here, everyone drives in the dead centre of the road at all times.*
>
> *Jilli: Oh and here but I do it properly... most of the time.*
>
> *Janet: So I sit in the middle of the car then? Oh no! How do I reach the steering wheel when I'm driving? Are the pedals on the same side as the steering wheel?*

# TAKE THREE BIRDS

*Jilli: I can do the gears, if you steer, but I will need a bottle of wine before we set off.*

*Janet: I think there's been a misunderstanding. When you emailed me originally saying did I like driving, I thought we were going to play golf. Oh well, not much difference.*

*Tottie: So pleased I'm not part of the road trip. If you reach me without getting arrested it will be a ruddy miracle.*

*Jilli: Haha FFS leave the shotgun at home, Farmer Bird!*

*Janet: I thought I'd be driving a tractor. Disappointed now. If you hit something when driving a tractor you just go straight over it. Simples.*

*Tottie: Are we sure they're even going to let Farmer Bird on a plane without a carer in attendance?*

*Janet: Do you think the driver will let me have a go at driving the plane? I'll ask.*

*Jilli: I think she might get arrested at passport control, so we may get out of this after all.*

*Janet: Has Jilli been in Police hands before? Hope she's not going to show me up!*

*Jilli: I wish! I would love to be in handcuffs, with a man in uniform.*

*Janet: Just stick with me - it won't be long*

*Tottie: Shurrup you two, am trying to write a serious letter to my lawyer in the very flowery French you have to use. Nothing to worry your pretty little heads about - I'm just taking out an injunction preventing you from entering the Auvergne.*

*Janet: Flowery French? Hope it's gluten free.*

*Tottie: You too are impossible! And it's even worse as these mails are coming out of synch for some reason so I am getting very confused here.*

*Janet: YOU TOO...!!!!!! Jilli - do you realise our book is being edited by this person!!! YOU TWO.....!!!!!*

*Jilli: I know, I know, half of it will be in French as well.*

*Janet: I'll leave the shotgun but unfortunately I'm going to have to bring my finger with me. I tried to chop it off - its healing now but the nail's black and handing off. If you're both nice to me I promise not to show it to you.*

*Tottie: Handing off? HANDING??? <harrumph>*

*Janet: Touché!!!!!!*

*Tottie: You're both touched, that's what worries me ;)*

*Jilli: Oh feck, I'm the only one that speaks English, we are doomed!*

## later via email ...

*Janet: Jilli's gone terribly quiet. I think she's trying to think of an excuse to get out of this.*

*Jilli: Jilli's waiting for nail varnish to dry, going out with a man (friend) tonight, then was supposed to have rendezvous with another later (lover) but as usual he let me down, wish I hadn't bothered to shave my legs now. Twatty bollox!*

*Tottie: You sure you speak English, Bird??*

*Jilli: More of a Yorkshire turrets if I'm honest. I swear I'd get more sex if I was married, why am I even bothering?*

*Tottie: Turrets???*

*Janet: Yeah - I think she's referring to a wall she wants me to build!*

*Jilli: Fecking spellchecker's fault, obviously I meant Tourettes, but if you want to build me a fortress at Pennington Palace then crack on bird.*

*Janet: Right - I'm putting an end to this foolishness as I'm taking my three English dogs for a walk across the field. Oooooh - a woman's just gone past with a French poodle. Arghhhhhh!*

*Jilli: And I'm going to iron my hair. Ciao for now birds. Oh yeah forgot to tell you my 18 year old car spontaneously combusted the other night, while the mechanic was towing it to the scrap yard. Don't worry I have replaced it with a 20 year old one, so we will definitely get there!*

*Tottie:Whaaaaaat?? Please tell me you are 'avin' a larf??*

*Janet: I know we've talked about burning up the road on this trip – but that's going a bit far! I'm going to increase my fire insurance – handy for a bar-b-que at the side of the road though.*

*Jilli - Oh also the new one is a GPL (gas) car and Fiat Puntos often burst into flames apparently (so I'm told, now I just bought my second one) but it all adds to the excitement, don't you think? Imagine the stories we will write - if we survive!*

*Tottie: Erm, just flagging up the minor factor that there are not many GPL service stations in this remote neck of the woods. But knowing you, you have already converted it to run on wine and there is plenty of that around here.*

*Janet: Is it really a gas car? My imagination's running wild – do you have Calor cylinders strapped to the back? Hey – we can have a bar-b-que while we're travelling. GPL = Generally Pissed Ladies.*

*Jilli - Who you calling a lady?*

*Tottie: I've just remembered – I'm moving house. The day before your visit!*

*Janet: no problem - have Calor, will travel! We can track you down anywhere and be with you in minutes.*

*Tottie: Huh! I have ex-military friends who call me GI Tottie for my backwoodsman skills. You'll never find me.*

*Jilli - Yes we will cos I borrowed a Pratnav!*

*Janet: Ok - we'll just break into your house and wait for your return. Leave plenty of wine for Jilli in fridge please.*

*Tottie: Then I really do have nothing to fear. With one of those instruments of the devil, you'll probably finish up in Paris. Or Calais. With any luck!*

# Chapter Six
# Feathering Nests

Jilli

Well, Farmer Bird is due and I am not even a little bit ready. I know she lives in a caravan and doesn't expect a mini-fridge or soap and a shower cap on her pillow, but I would like at least to have time to rearrange the cobwebs and fill the wine rack. Oh and I may have to clean inside the car. Don't want to give a bad first impression, I will probably do that just by opening my mouth.

I have two clients' houses to clean this week, a shower wall to tile, a taxi run to do, oh and the car needs a service, and if I don't cut the grass she won't even find the house. I also rather stupidly agreed to visit a friend in another part of Italy the weekend before her arrival, which I really want to do but not sure if there are enough hours to do it all.

I wonder if it's too late to cancel!

So first things first, decide where she's sleeping. Goat Cottage (my converted animal shed/glamping barn) is very cosy and spacious but it will feel like putting the guest in the garden shed, and I would like to get to know her a bit before our adventure. It may be best to put her in the office/bedroom I think. Although last time my daughter put her head around the door, looking for the printer, she said 'It looks like an episode of Hoarders in here!' So that clearly needs attending to - when

I get a minute.

I seem to be spending half the day on the internet checking emails to see if this is all really going to happen. It seems it is!

Me and my daft ideas! I am excited, apprehensive, and stressed all at the same time. What if it all goes wrong? What if we don't like each other? Tottie is getting it easy, she only has to suffer us for three days, but me and Farmer Bird are stuck with each other for a whole week and two of those days we are going to be in a car together. We will either end up killing each other or getting married!

And then there's the car. It's a twenty-year-old Fiat Punto. I only bought it recently because the last one burst into flames. That one was only eighteen years old, what if this one does the same en-route?

Stop panicking, Doris, and get your arse into gear. Buy food. No, buy wine. No, buy food and wine, but mainly wine. I know already that Farmer Bird likes a little drink so at least we have something in common. Oh crap, I have no money!

I love cooking but as her plane lands late we will need to eat out on the first night. The one thing I wanted to make for her was Provençal chicken, basically a one-pot chicken with olive oil and loads of garlic. It is one of my favourite dishes at the moment and rather fitting as I got the recipe from Tottie, so I will do that the second night.

Must also fill the freezer for the teenager while I am 'AWOL' otherwise she may starve. Fill the dog food cupboard or the dogs will starve. Gawd, I will need a holiday after all this. Just realised I still haven't paid the electricity bill, must try to find money for that otherwise teenager and dogs will be in the dark.

Oh crap, I need to pack as well. How did I manage to forget about this? On my passport it says Jilli 'Hermit' Pennington as I rarely travel, pretty much never go anywhere, (apart from this month) so when it comes to packing I usually arrive at my destination and find I have forgotten to bring important stuff like clothes and shoes.

I don't own many clothes so Tottie has offered to lend wet weather gear if I need it (got to forty-seven years old and haven't yet. I stay in if it rains. Simple.) and apart from that I will probably just pack everything I own to be on the safe side. At least going by car I don't have to worry about weight and size of my luggage.

When people visit here I usually take them to the top of a big flat mountain called Bismantova. It looks huge but only actually takes twenty minutes to get from the car park to the top, and it's well worth the hike. So if we get a nice day I will drag Farmer Bird up there.

Another thing I like to do for 'first timers' is introduce them to a local speciality ( not usually found in other regions of Italy) called 'Erbazzone'. It's a flat savoury pasty filled with spinach and Parmesan, and is the most addictive thing to eat, even people who wouldn't normally like spinach tend to love it.

Emilia Romagna is the food capital of Italy and it has for me been one of the delights of living here. Unlike areas of Italy that are 'touristy', our restaurants tend to cater for local people, so they care about pleasing you and go out of their way to make sure you have a good meal as, unlike tourists, they know if they feed you well that you will return. Also their prices are tailored for locals rather than tourists so you don't get a nasty shock at the end as you might in Tuscany or Venice.

I like to take my guests to the local restaurants to sample the amazing food that the region has to offer, but Farmer Bird is only here for one day either side of the France trip so it will be difficult to fit everything in. Maybe if we become 'proper' friends she will visit again and I can get to show off a bit more.

Tottie

I love planning! I always get just as much fun from planning any event as from the event itself. This wild scheme to meet up with the other birds is no exception. As soon as I knew that it was a goer, on went the thinking cap to consider such important things as menus, accommodation and trips out.

Accommodation was easy. I'm a big kid at heart, I love camping in all weathers, even sleeping out in a tent in my garden sometimes. My big tent goes up there for much of the summer and the dogs and I spend our nights in it. So that means, with two empty bedrooms in the house, Jilli and Farmer Bird can have one each. As they will have spent something like eight or more hours in a very small car together on the drive here from Italy, having never previously met, they might be glad of a bit of space!

I love cooking, and especially planning what to cook for my visitors. I always like to give them a taste of the very good local produce. The Auvergne isn't widely known, it remains one of France's secret, unspoilt corners, but at one time, no decent restaurant in Paris would be without an Auvergnat chef and the produce is still highly rated, and rightly so.

I know Jilli hates cooked bananas and fennel – strange combination – but Farmer Bird reckons she will eat anything I put in front of her. I may just call her bluff and try her with Époisse cheese, although it's not a local one. It's a variety so pungent it is actually prohibited on all forms of public transport in France.

Meals in the Auvergne are usually copious and hearty, and four course meals are the norm, with cheese being served between the main course and the dessert.

My current favourite dish to make for visitors whose arrival time is uncertain is actually a southern French dish from Provence. I hope neither of them was being polite when they said they like garlic. It's called chicken with forty cloves of garlic, and that's not a typing error. It's great in that it can be stuck in the oven and left to it without risk of spoiling if the intrepid travellers are unavoidably delayed.

Farmer Bird seems very capable of sorting herself out but is our Doris, I ask myself? Will the two of them manage to get from one country to another without causing an international incident and getting themselves arrested?

I must remember to tell them about public loos in France, although they may be the same in Italy. Here they are often mixed and many new visitors to France have come bolting out of the door of public conveniences very quickly on discovering themselves confronted by a row of urinals and getting a 'bonjour' from the totally unconcerned French man or men using them.

My little grottage is at eighteen hundred feet in a wild and wooded region on the eastern edge of the Auvergne, known as the Livradois Forez. If you're local, you pronounce the Z at the end, if you're not, you don't. Being central continental, it is rather prone to thunderstorms at the best of times but Mother Nature seemed to have redoubled her efforts as soon as the trip was arranged and Farmer Bird's flight booked. Perhaps she is trying to tell me something!

I'm very proud of my adopted region, love showing it off to people who've never been, so I'm really hoping the weather gods will be kind enough to let me show my visitors some of the wonderful views without risking getting them struck by lightning.

Although, who knows, after a short time in their company, that might seem like a good idea!

By coincidence, their arrival date falls on the day of our local village fête, which always ends in a small but spectacular firework display set against the backdrop of a modest château perched on top of a hill.

Rural French attitude to health and safety comes as something of a shock to those from the much more nanny-like state of the UK. At the same event last year, with bizarre men letting off fireworks they held in their hands and splashing burning spirit everywhere, the only sign of any measure to prevent the crowd from spontaneously combusting was the mayor carrying a five-litre garden weed spray full of tap water.

If the Birds find their way here, if they don't get arrested, if Doris's dodgy little car makes the trip and if their estimate of driving time is correct – and that's an awful lot of Ifs - we should be able to enjoy tea and cake on arrival, a dog walk round the hamlet, a leisurely supper and still have time to take in the fireworks. My main preparations will be the culinary kind, making cake, sourcing some local produce they may not have tried before, and prepping desserts and vegetables. If they're very lucky, I may find time to whiz round with a vacuum cleaner so the rugs don't all look like mohair.

I should be successfully able to mask the permanent smell of dog by dint of a cunning plan. I've bought them posh guest soaps from our local artisan soap maker, which smell divine, so hopefully they won't notice the dog smell. Especially as my dogs are fed on what is called the BARF diet – bones and raw food. You try sharing living space with raw cabbage-fuelled dogs and see how you like it.

So the cake is baked, a gluten free loaf of bread (I use the term loosely – they all taste like cardboard) is baked for me, as I have Coeliac disease, although I shall allow my guests to eat locally made and very good *baguettes, croissants, pain au chocolate* etc (sob, sob), bedding is sorted and one guest bed is made up, with the other to finish.

All I have to do now is to wait, and to wonder, if and when they will arrive.

And then fate, as if often the case, landed a bit of a body blow, less than a week before the Birds were due to arrive with me, and just three days before Farmer Bird Janet started on the first leg of her journey.

My beloved dog Ci, just eight years old, was suddenly taken critically ill with breathing difficulties and, despite the best efforts of the emergency vet on duty, in less than twenty-four hours, he was dead.

Even a professional wordsmith like me could not find the way adequately to express my grief at his sudden loss, the huge gaping hole in my life his passing made. The last thing in the world I wanted to do was spend time with people, certainly not with anyone who was not already a very close friend. I was still at the stage of dissolving into tears at the least little thing and I am not someone who cries easily in the company of others, even of close friends.

And yet, and yet. We had all already invested so much in this trip. Janet had bought her plane ticket, on a low-cost service. Even if she had taken out expensive travel insurance, which I doubted, it was highly unlikely that any insurer would pay out for cancellation or altered flights on the basis of the death of a dog, even one who meant as much to me as Ci did.

There was also the book itself. We'd set ourselves a pretty punishing schedule of getting it written and published before Christmas, barely three months in total. It was doable, just, but not if we delayed the meeting. We were all agreed that there was to be no cheating with the book. We would only write about real life events, so if Jilli and Janet met up but didn't come to me, there would be no pretending they had and writing a fictional version of that part of the trip.

It was all so sudden, my feelings were still so raw, but in a strange way, I wondered if this visit from two virtual strangers might be just what I needed to stick a temporary plaster over my wounds.

Both my visitors were doggy people, both had doubtless lost adored dogs themselves in the past and would certainly understand what I was feeling.

Ci was to be cremated, then his ashes would be coming home to be scattered under the silver birch tree I had planted ready to receive my own mortal remains in due course. I would not be getting him back until after my visitors had been and gone.

Perhaps it was time to put my feelings on ice, welcome my

guests, then do my grieving in private after they had gone and my boy came home for the last time.

Janet

I need to book my flight, get a boarding pass and some Euros. I need a suitcase as well and I need to check about weight limits on what you can pack. I'm running round like a headless chicken. Heaven knows what it would be like if I was organising something complicated! I'm sure that to people who travel regularly all this must be just simple preparation, but as I've never flown before I'm pretty much in the dark about everything I'm doing.

Tottie wants me to take her some gluten free biscuits so I'll have a hunt for those as well. I'm really looking forward to this holiday. I use the word holiday but Jilli says oh no, it's not a holiday. So heaven knows how much work I'm going to be doing, but I'm viewing it as a holiday and really looking forward to it.

I've never been to Italy or France or anywhere else come to that, apart from one school holiday in Switzerland. I'm very excited, really keen to experience my first flight, and of course to meeting Jilli and then Tottie. Hopefully we'll get along as well as we seem to be doing via our emails and we'll all have a whale of a time.

Unfortunately I heard from Tottie just two days before my flight that one of her dogs had died and obviously that's a very sad situation. I've been there lots of times myself and I know how painful it is. It's one of those things, life and death.

I don't know how Tottie deals with things like that and whether a visit by two rather moronic people to stay for a few days will help or hinder. I know if I lost one of my dogs right now I wouldn't want to see anybody or speak to anybody or do anything for several days. Perhaps that's not the best way of dealing with grief, but it's my way. Maybe Tottie just doesn't want to ask us to delay our trip as it's so close or maybe having a couple of people stay for a day or two will help her through a few days. I don't know, but I do feel for her.

I'd agreed to go on this adventure all of a sudden without any warning so here I am faced with never having travelled very much, never having been on a plane, never having been abroad by myself, never having spoken any other languages, so it's all going to be a bit of a challenge.

The first thing I had to do of course was get a passport. The only thing I knew about getting a passport was that this last year there's been a lot of hoo-ha about the British passport service being in a mess and having great big backlogs. I've seen on telly about people having to cancel holidays because of time problems. One or two friends warned me not to book my flight until I had got my passport.

I wanted to get the trip done soon as I didn't want to go away and leave my dogs in the caravan with no heating on when we got into October or November. When the idea was put to me in August the weather was still nice and warm but it could start to get colder any time now. I have a log burner in the caravan but only have it lit when I'm there – it would be dangerous to leave the dogs on their own with the stove lit and I can't expect my friends to be lighting the stove and supervising it as well as looking after my dogs. It was already nearing the end of September so time was pretty limited.

I checked out what I needed to do to get a passport, tried to do it online and got in a muddle. Then I discovered you could get the form from the Post Office for about eight pounds and they would check the form for you before it went off to make sure that it was right. I thought that was the best way so I cancelled my application online and went to get the form from the Post Office and had a read.

I realised that you had to have someone who's known you for a minimum of two years to sign your form. They have to have a passport of their own and they have to be a professional person. So the first challenge was to find someone like that.

Luckily some friends I do work for on a Sunday, mucking out their horses, fitted the bill and they agreed to help me and do the necessary on my form. I then trotted off back to the Post Office and handed it over to the man behind the counter.

He looked through it then handed it back and said: 'Oh no, no, do it again.' It appeared that in signing my signature, I'd read that you have to keep it within the box on the form and I thought I had done so. But it turned out that on the very last letter, the T of Holt, the cross bar on the letter was just microscopically touching the line of the box. Apparently that is sufficient for the computer to spit it out and say no it's wrong.

So the man gave me the form back and said do it again and this time don't just stay in the box, don't even touch any of the lines. It might have helped if the form had said that! I had to go home and fill it all in again very carefully. Of course the more conscious I was of how careful I had to be, the more difficult it was. I took absolutely ages!

Then I realised my friend would have to fill in his bit again as although it had been perfect on the first form, he had to do it again, the same as me, on the new form. So we both did our bits again and back I trotted once more to the Post Office.

I'd had my picture done in one of those booths where you just put your money in and sit while the photos are taken. I'd got four pictures of me, wonderful portraits, I thought, but then the man said I couldn't use those pictures, 'Because you're smiling. You're not allowed to smile.' I would have to go and get some more.

I wasn't smiling by then, I can tell you that. Luckily just opposite the Post Office was a photographic shop so I went in there and told them what the problem was. The lady said they would do the photographs and make absolutely sure they were right. So I paid over more money and she began, but she kept saying to me: 'Don't smile!' So with my new photographs in one hand and my new form in the other, I went back to the Post

Office for the third time and the man sighed, then checked everything and said it was all in order but that it would probably take six weeks. He also told me not to book the flight until I had the passport.

Then after a few weeks I got a letter asking me to go for an identity interview at Sheffield Passport Office, which I did. That was a little bit like being in the hands of the police, once you got into the office, because it's all divided into offices which are completely sealed up, with bulletproof glass and doors which lock.

You're taken into reception and the doors are all locked, then about six of you are taken into another holding area where the doors are again locked behind you and there are no windows and I thought it was like being in prison. Then you're taken to a booth and interviewed, basically to check that you are who you say you are.

At the end of it all the nice, polite man who had interviewed me advised me that everything seemed to be in order and the passport would be posted to me within the next four or five days. That was a Friday and in fact the passport arrived the following Tuesday, which was very good. It arrived in less than six weeks, so well done the Passport Office.

The next thing I had to do was sort out some Euros for the trip. I'd asked a few people for advice, whether to get Euros on the other side of the Channel, or before I went, or whether to use my card. I went online and found a good rate but for far more Euros than I wanted for just a week.

I went to various places like building societies and the Post Office looking for the best rate, which seemed to be the Post Office. I'd left it a bit to the last minute and I didn't know if you had to order them in advance. On the way to the Post Office I got stuck in roadworks and arrived just as they'd pulled down the blinds and of course they couldn't reopen for little old me. So I had to go all the way back through the roadworks and then go back again the following day.

Thankfully, for the amount I needed, I was just able to walk in and buy them, I didn't have to order them and then go back another day. But of course it turned out that buying them like that over the counter I didn't get as good a deal as I thought I was getting.

From there I popped across to the Co-op shop for a bit of last minute shopping and discovered that I could have bought my Euros there, conveniently made up in packs of one hundred and at a better rate! Of course that's the shop I go to day in, day out for my shopping and I've never before seen that they sell Euros.

So, Euros safely in pocket, it was back home to sort out the best flight and of course, that was now much more expensive than when I had been looking while I waited for my passport to arrive. Something to do with an air traffic controllers' strike a few days before causing a backlog.

This was my first experience of booking a flight online and when I got to the checkout I discovered you get offered all sorts of extras, a bit of this, a bit of that and the other. But I did notice you could pay for priority boarding and for choosing your own seat.

As I'd never flown before, I did want to be able to see out of a window. I hate being amongst crowds of people and feeling trapped, but felt I would be able to deal with the enforced confinement if I could see out of a window. A plan of the plane came up, so I chose what I thought was a window seat just in front of the wing and paid the extra two pounds to book that particular seat.

Then I decided to pay another two pounds for priority boarding and to make sure my cabin bag stayed with me. I didn't really know how it all worked but I printed out my boarding pass and it all seemed simple and straightforward.

So now here I am, all set, and case all packed. I bought myself a brand new case from a shop which showed which cases were suitable for which airline, by dimension. And now

# FEATHERING NESTS

I'm all ready for the off. My flight leaves in one week's time from Manchester Airport.

**via email**

> *Tottie: I am busy thinking up filthy foreign food to serve you and deciding if you merit the best antique bed linen or scabby old nylon sheets and hairy horse blankets.*
>
> *Janet: Here's a challenge for you - I bet I can eat anything you put in front of me (provided it's food). Hairy old horse blankets will do me fine. They'll match my hairy old body.*

**later ...**

> *Janet: WELL! I've never spent so much time and effort trying to get money. Having decided best deal is with Post Office I went to Bakewell this am to buy some. Bloody roadworks. I arrived at PO just as they were closing the counter. AND of course they couldn't possibly stay open for two more minutes even though they agreed the roadworks are causing mayhem!!!! Arghhhh. So I've come home with fish and chips!*
>
> *Tottie: Tee-hee, this is going to be brilliant material for the book, you're clearly as much of a walking disaster area as I am. You're not on Facebook much so may not have seen that yesterday I fell through some rotten floorboards in my hayloft and it was only that one leg and the opposite foot got bent back and jammed which stopped me falling through. So I now have a toe to match your finger - I hate to be outdone.*

# TAKE THREE BIRDS

*Janet: Oh well done. You can still cook with broken legs you know! So. Back to the post office on Monday am. Of course the roadworks will still be there plus there's a big agricultural market on a Monday so I'll probably not be back till Tuesday. Then I'll have to go back to pick Euros up. Arghhhhh.*

*And, having just had a practice run and packed my suitcase I've had to throw a few things out to fit everything in. (I'm only bringing a cabin bag so it's a bit limited). I've ditched the Parka and replaced with a bikini. That seems to have sorted it. Plus I've got to keep it under ten kilos so I may have to eat Tottie's gluten free biscuits. I also wish I hadn't decided to tidy my caravan so that when I come back it's all done. Hell's bells - I've been cleaning and sorting since first thing this morning and it now looks like a bomb site.*

*Tottie: I can easily lend you ladies coats and waterproofs etc. I have the European collection of bargains from all the vide greniers (attic sales) I go to.*

*Jilli: Well I can bring everything I own, as long as it fits in the car, but have no outdoor gear, as I stay in if the weather is shite. I will definitely need to borrow.*

*Janet: So....if the weather's shite me and Jilli stay indoors, eat Tottie's food and drink wine. Tottie can put on her waterproofs and go for a walk then spend the night in her tent. Itinerary sorted.*

*Jilli: Shh! she'll move house before we get there.*

*Tottie: Anyway, what food?? You think you'll find food here?*

*Janet: Hey Jilli. Not looking good. How about we stay at yours and drink wine for a few days?*

*Tottie: Pair of total lushes!*

**later, via email:**

*Janet: Only 48 hours to go!!!*

*Jilli: Oh god, is it this week?*

*Janet: Please don't call me god. Your Ladyship will do. Don't forget to tug your forelock.*

*Tottie: <groan> the old ones are always the best.*

*Jilli: Hope so, that's why I am going on hols with two pensioners!*

*Janet: Cheek!*

*Tottie: You get her first, Farmer Bird, so you get to box her ears first.*

*Janet: We'll have welly boots at fifty paces.*

*Tottie: She can't count that far.*

*Janet: Welly funny!*

**later, via email ...**

*Jilli: Just to keep you both updated. My car got to Umbria and back to visit a friend (4 hrs each way) with no problems. Then when I filled it with gas yesterday they told me it had a slow leak in the tank. So I'm taking it in this afternoon to see if they can sort it out. At this point I believe it is just a valve and is solvable reasonably quick and cheap, but I am always optimistic. If I need to panic I will do that later.*

*Janet: That sounds good, apart from the leak, but I'll bring some chewing gum with me! I'm good for driving, changing wheels, changing filters, changing oil and water and generally staring at engines and going 'Mmmm'. I can also push quite hard. We could always cycle, but by the time we got to Tottie's it'd be time to turn round and go back.*

*Tottie: Good luck with the car! Is there a plan B if not?? Getting exciting now! Just hope the rain holds off for the fireworks in my village on Saturday as they are always good, would be nice to take you.*
*PS Red or white wine birds? Am going shopping today so will get you a glass between you to have with your dry crusts of bread.*

*Janet: Plan B? Oh no, no, no. That would spoil the trip. Never have a plan B. We'll just jump in Jilli's car and drive - well that's the first five hundred metres done. That should enable us to whip up some interest in the book.*

*Tots: Getting concerned now that Farmer Bird is talking about whippings already! What about the vino, birds, red or white? Remember I can't have more than a thimbleful of the falling down water, so it's just you birds who will be on the lash.*

*Janet: Re Tottie's postscript - dry crusts of bread.*

*Don't take the title of the book too literally Tottie! And no I don't like worms - cooked or otherwise!*

*Jilli: Red, white, pink, I will drink.*

*Janet: Whine. I'm not much of a 'conasewer' but generally prefer white. Thanks. Well I may have to use the whip when Jilli is pulling her car up mountain passes. I've now got my Euros and still have some money left in my account. My next pension payment is on the Thursday I fly back, so I'll have funds that morning. J. Rockefeller.*

*Tottie: Feck, with all that money you don't think either of us will be letting you go back, do you??*

*Janet: Just so long as you can keep me in the manner to which I'm accustomed!*

*Jilli: So far so good then, now back to scrubbing my house for the guest!*

*Tottie: Very Important!! Don't forget if we do have storms here I will have no internet and therefore no phone. My mobile doesn't get a signal inside the house but you can text me and I can receive that, though not always send a reply. Just so you can keep in touch on the journey and let me know when you have been arrested - so I can pee myself laughing.*

*Janet: You're really expecting us to make it to France then? There's optimism for you. Stop talking - Jilli's mowing her legs, she says.*

*Tottie: <vomit>*

*Janet: Have you checked she's actually Human? I would have questions about someone who mows their legs every day. We're not writing a Werewolf novel I hope. I need to go and check the moon cycles over the next week.*

*Jilli: If we don't all get along (and that is a possibility you know) I suggest we set the camera rolling, have a massive punch up and put it on YouTube.*

*Tottie: You really think we will have to stage the punch-up??*

*Jilli: Yes but you will have to get drunk first to get into the right frame of mind. I will bring the thimble.*

*Janet: Tottie - if you've got a mud hole outside I suggest we all strip and have the punch up there. That'll sell. Plus the mud will hide your and Jilli's wrinkles.*

**later, via email:**

*Jilli: Car man fixed my car for ten Euro, no plan B needed, he just had a fiddle underneath with a tube and job's a gud un!*

*Tottie: So you're definitely coming then? Feck! Send me a text when you turn off the A89 motorway then I will know your estimated time of arrival approximately so the dog and I can feck off somewhere and change the locks.*

*Janet: MOTORWAY? Hell-fire, I had visions of tootling along on picturesque Fritalian lanes - not tear-arsing down a motorway. What about mountain passes - any of those?*

*Tottie: Don't tell me, you're looking for a lonely goatherd? The A89 is a fab motorway, very little traffic and stunning views. But there are often vultures just near where you turn off so try not to linger too long.*

*Jilli: Haha, if it's mountain passes you are after you will be vomiting on our hairpin bends in no time.*

*Janet: Do we have to take a canoe down any creeks with locals who sit playing 'Duelling Banjos'?*

*Tottie: Nar, here they just shoot you first, they don't waste time with any of that faff.*

*Janet: That's alright then. I'll sit Jilli on the roof-rack as a decoy.*

# Chapter Seven
# Taking Flight

**via email ...**

*Tottie: You two birds better bring your own Yorkshire tea. I've gone native, I only drink weak wimbly weasel water. You can't get anything stronger than Lipton's yellow label here anyway*

*Janet: And - what's the weather doing in Fritaly? Do I need warm, cool or intermediate clothes?*

*Jilli: Just had scorchio morning and hail stones as big as golf balls this aft, thought my windscreen was going. Bring jeans/shorts/t-shirts/fleece or jumper and jacket to be on safe side. Don't bother with the bikini though!*

*Janet: Bugger. I was going to travel over in my bikini!*

*Tottie: A word about our weather - you could get all four seasons in one day here. Bring layers. We're at 1800 feet so the evenings are getting chilly, unless I crank up Kevin the Kitchen Range. And we do get rain, it's not the green heart of France for nothing. Will give you an update at the last minute. On the other hand, it was nearly 30 degrees in the shade yesterday before the storm broke.*

*Janet: Bugger - take fur coat out of suitcase!!!*

*Tottie: Predicting Auvergnat weather is like trying to smell the colour nine.*

*Janet: Oh, I quite like the smell of nine. It's five I can't stand.*

*Tottie: There's a déviation (diversion) just before you get to me at the moment, for bridge repairs, so I'll keep you posted on that. It's very easy to bring you in a slightly different way for the last five miles or so - just don't whatever you do follow their déviation signs as they take you miles out then abandon you in the forest - I went to check them out today.*

*Janet: Ok well I will just be glad if we find France! As soon as I see a bloke with an onion necklace and a beret, I will relax, pull over and say ' Bonjour, does tha know where Tottie's gaff is, mate?' It's getting very close now!*

*Tottie: Don't worry Farmer Bird, the deafening silence from Doris is not trepidation about your arrival, it's just all her frisky nocturnal activity resulted in the bed collapsing.*

*Jilli: Yes and if I don't fix it, we may be sharing a bed.*

*Janet: Now the silence is coming from me! I've just been checking I can use the movie making feature on my camera as I've not used it before. It's brilliant -*

*really clear when rerun on computer. I'll bring the charger with me so we've plenty of running time -- do you have an adapter for a British standard 3 pin plug? Presumably it won't just plug into your socket.*

*Tottie: I have adaptificators, doubt Doris is that organised ;)*

*Janet: Well how wrong can you be! Doris has just confirmed she's got two.*

*Tottie: Oooooh, get her ;)*

*Jilli: I assume you mean electric sockets - Europe to UK?*

*Janet: Yes, electric. Although gas sockets will do at a pinch.*

*Tottie: PMSL!*

*Janet: Oh. Pre Menstrual Super Link. Right.*

*Tottie: You two crack me up. P\*ssing Myself Laughing that Doris asked about electrical sockets and Janet said gas would do.*

*Jilli: Don't see what's funny about that!*

*Tottie: It's funny that you didn't get why I was PMSL.*

*Jilli: We can laugh at each other!*

*Tottie: Oh you'll laugh when you see your accommodation, that's for sure. The dogs have a nice kennel and they say you're welcome to borrow that.*

*Janet: Oh no, no, no. If anyone's getting kicked out it's that eagle with stubby feet!*

*Tottie: I'll be sleeping in the tent. It's the most comfortable accommodation there is.*

*Jilli: Hey - I'm not coming over there to sleep. I'm expecting wild parties lasting all night. Zzzzzzzz ........*

Jilli

So the day of Farmer Bird's arrival was finally here. I had cleaned the house, got the wine in the fridge, filled the car with gas and was ready to go. Proper excited like a child and couldn't believe we are all going to meet at last.

Then one of my clients contacted me to see if I could do a last minute clean as she had a booking for the following Friday. I thought that meant the Friday after the France trip, but no, it meant the Friday when I would be in France, so I said yes anyway as I never turn work down and rushed off to the property to get it ready. I spent the day razzing around like a muppet getting the house cleaned, beds made and grass cut, only to arrive home to an email saying the ignorant moron had cancelled their booking. And with no deposit paid my client was now out of pocket and I had wasted half my day doing something totally pointless.

My daughter Millie decided she would come to the airport with me to collect Janet, then we could do photos and a meet-up video. But obviously her being a teen-thing, I had my coat on and my car keys in my hand while she was still faffing about with make-up and hair straighteners.

Farmer Bird sent me a text to say her plane had taken off about twenty minutes late so I figured I could do a quick detour to the big DIY shop near the airport, only the stupid pilot put his foot down and brought the bird down on time. I was just getting back onto the autostrada (motorway) when a message came in saying Farmer Bird just landed.

Brilliant, I thought, she has flown to a different country for the first time, to meet a complete stranger and I am not going to bloody well be there! How did I manage to cock this up? She will be wandering around the airport wondering where the heck I am.

I put my foot down and overtook a police car in the slow lane. Whoops! It was ok he was busy texting someone and didn't notice me.

Got to the airport, no time for a pee-stop, went straight to the arrivals, and waited, and waited... Then Farmer Bird messaged me to say she was by the front door and had been there for ages, so we must have walked straight past each other.

Tottie

Well, all I can say is that I'm delighted it is the other two Birds doing this long journey and not me. I'm not kidding when I say I have to be prised, kicking and screaming, out of the Auvergne and the idea of any kind of long journey fills me with utter dread these days. By long journey, these days, I mean anything over about an hour.

I'm particularly relieved it's not me boarding a plane, since I hate flying so much. I have nothing but admiration for Janet jumping onto her first ever flight with less concern than if she were simply taking a bus to Matlock.

I have hated flying since my first ever flight, on an ancient Caravelle from Manchester to Paris, for a school exchange trip. I didn't expect to, I was quite excited at the prospect. But from the moment we started our rattling way down the runway and lumbered into a very ungainly climb, it was a total 'stop the world, I want to get off' moment for me, which has never left me with each subsequent flight.

It didn't help that we got caught up in the inevitable French air traffic controllers' strike, which seems to be a regular feature of French air travel, or that we had something of a comedian piloting the plane we were flying in.

We were supposed to be going to Paris's Orly airport, from where we would transfer to a train for our trip down to the Rhone valley, which was where the school ours was twinned with was located. I was utterly terrified for every minute of the flight so was very relieved when we started to circle and prepare for the approach into Orly.

One of the reasons I hate flying so much is I seem to have very sensitive middle ears. They are already screaming at me: 'OMG, we're going down!!' long before the captain has announced that we have begun our descent. So I was acutely aware that our circling was taking us not just down but then back up again.

Eventually the captain's voice came over the tannoy, full of apology, to say that because of strike action by air traffic controllers, we were being held in a queue and would have to keep circling for a bit longer. Our poor French mistress, who was in charge of this bunch of excitable young teenagers, was beside herself by now, knowing that we were running a grave risk of missing our train, on which we had reserved seats.

After what seemed to me an eternity, the captain said we had been offered a landing window at Le Bourget airport, also in Paris, a little sooner than Orly could accommodate us, so we were diverting there.

So it was back to going round and round and down, round and round and up, but this time over a different airport. By this stage I could actually see the runway below us from the window and felt like telling them just to open a door, I'd jump, anything to get back down on the ground.

It didn't help at all that our jovial captain told us that we had been allocated a slot to land in about ten minutes' time and quipped merrily: 'I think we have enough fuel to last us that long!' People keep telling me that the more you travel by air, the less it bothers you. I've now flown to Spain three times, France four times, Corsica twice, Gibraltar twice, Sweden once, the USA once and Canada once. If it's going to get any better, when will that be? So I've decided it's not for me, I'm not going to do it any more.

I've tried all sorts of remedies to rid me of my aerophobia, from being hypnotised, which felt more like a chance for a rather seedy bloke in a shed in his back garden in South Wales to put his paws all over me, to getting Valium from a sympathetic doctor. He told me I could take up to three but that three would probably knock me out, which sounded ideal to me. I took three, then another couple, then some more. I had seven in total which seemed to have absolutely no effect on my anxiety levels.

Anyway, my main excuse for refusing to budge was that, geographically, I was about halfway between Doris Bird in Italy and Farmer Bird in England, so it made sense for them to come to me and I was very grateful that they had agreed to do so.

There was also the question of my dogs. There was no way I would ever have gone away and left Ci in the care of someone else. He was a rescue dog with issues. Having been abandoned by his former owners, I had promised him that I would never leave him, not even for a short time.

I was amazed Jilli had agreed to travel, knowing she's as much of a hermit as I am. I'd never really thought about whether or not Janet was a traveller, though I doubted it, with her farming background.

Well done, Birds, for being the ones to agree to make the long road trip. I don't envy you, but I am eternally grateful to you both for your brave act which let me off have to travel anywhere by any means.

# TAKING FLIGHT

Janet

Because I hadn't flown before I kept checking my flight time, which terminal it went from at Manchester Airport, and that I had my ticket and boarding pass on my day of departure. My flight was due to leave at 2.45pm and the friend who owns the farm where I live very kindly offered to take me to the airport.

He has people who work for him who regularly fly abroad so he knows the airport well and knew instantly where to go. I had to be there two hours before the flight, which made it 12.45. I said I didn't mind at all if we got there early as I'd never been inside an airport before and thought I would probably make mistakes. I wanted to have time to wander about rather than panicking and being on the last minute.

We aimed to get there at midday so I would have plenty of time to get a coffee and relax. In fact we got there at about quarter to, he dropped me at the entrance to Terminal 3 and then said: 'There you are, it's all down to you now,' before driving away and leaving me to it.

I went into the airport and stood staring about, probably looking like a lost soul. But it all seemed quite straightforward, I could see a great long line of check-in desks in front of me, and at the end I could see Ryanair, which was the one I needed.

There were tapes up and people queuing and only one Ryanair attendant there. I thought that was obviously the first place to go and headed there. Then I saw a machine that offered to weigh your case, which I thought was a good idea, as I'd only managed to weigh mine on the bathroom scales I hadn't used for years as I don't usually bother weighing myself. It came in at nine and a half kilos and the allowance was ten.

I thought that was a bit close, what if I got to check-in and it was over weight? So I'd pulled out some stuff to bring the weight down a bit just to be sure. I had a fleece coat to wear and another in my case, as Tottie had said it could be cold at her place at night. So I'd taken the one out of my case and was wearing that as well as the other one, over the top of my blouse.

I'm sure I must have looked like I was having a heart attack while waiting at the airport. I was sweating profusely and the sweat was running down my face and dripping off my chin. But heigh-ho, I was saving a bit of weight in my baggage and losing some myself into the bargain!

When I put my case on the machine at the airport it came in at just six kilos so I'd had no need to throw anything out. Obviously my bathroom scales were a bit out! I didn't want to start stripping off and repacking my case in the middle of the airport so I decided to just look as if I was ill and at least I would get some sympathy!

Then I looked at the monitor and found my flight to Bologna listed, but I noticed that it gave the time as 16.45, four forty-five, not two forty-five as I had thought not being used to the twenty-four hour clock. So I wasn't at the airport three hours early, which would have been more than enough, but five hours early. Never mind! Loads of time to make mistakes, and plenty of time to sit in a café and have some lunch – better than being late.

There was a man going past with some luggage so I explained to him I'd never been in an airport before and asked where I had to go. He asked who I was flying with then he pointed to the Ryanair desk and said I had to go over there and queue up.

That's what I had thought and that seemed easy. Then I couldn't actually find the entrance into the maze, approaching the desk, the tapes zig-zagging towards the desks. I could see the people in the queue I wanted to join but I couldn't seem to find the entrance. It was a bit like those mazes on the back of a cornflake packet.

I went in one entrance and zig-zagged all the way down

then found myself in the wrong place, so I had to zig-zag all the way back. I did think of hurdling the tape just to join the queue but then thought perhaps that wasn't the right thing to do.

Eventually I found the way to join the right queue, with only about six people in front of me, though very slow moving. I stood and waited and waited, watching them showing their passports and things and getting papers in return from the lady, then putting their bags on the belt, so I would know what to do when it was my turn.

I shuffled forward behind everyone else and eventually they'd all gone through and it was just me and the Ryan Air lady behind the desk. I had my passport and my boarding pass in my hand and I held them up. She looked at them and took my boarding pass, looked at it again and asked me if I had checked in online.

I said I wasn't sure - I'd got my boarding pass online. She explained that was what she meant by checking in online and that since I had done that I did not need to queue up there, I could just go through the gates over there, straight through to departures.

Oops! So I took my stuff back from her and walked away. I must say the lady was extremely polite, she said thank you and goodbye and she didn't add 'you stupid moron' which I'm sure was what she was thinking.

So I zig-zagged my way back through the maze and trundled off to the departure gate. I kept looking at all the monitors and managed to suss out what was going on and, with three hours still to wait, I found a café, had some lunch and a cup of tea. Someone had kindly left a current newspaper in the café so I picked it up and spent some time reading and then – another cup of tea!

Then it was time to board the plane, which was very simple.

Anyone reading this must think 'what an idiot' but when you've never been in an airport before and you've got all the people milling about and all the monitors, it's a bit confusing until you know the procedure. Plus, I can get a bit panicky in crowds of people so it actually helped me to have so much time to spare as, if necessary, I could go outside and have a walk round and then return inside, without fear of missing my flight.

I found my seat on the plane, put my bag in the cabin hold then wondered what was going on. Despite my careful studying of the seating plan online, I had got the only seat on the plane without any window at all. I never did suss out why it was missing, it was just the side of the plane, in front of the wing. On the same row of seats on the other side of the aisle there was a window. So out of however many seats there were on the plane, I'd managed to pick the one and only one without a window for my first flight. Well done, Janet.

I'd looked carefully on the plan and had seen a little square thing which I thought was a window but it turned out to be an arm-rest! I couldn't see anything very much through the arm-rest but the flight went perfectly well. I didn't feel any nervousness or apprehension about flying for the first time and I coped with the close proximity of all the other passengers without any problem.

Once we'd taken off and were flying, because I couldn't see outside, I actually found it a little bit boring and I was glad when we landed. The entry into Italy all went smoothly, I just walked through passport control waving my passport around and there I was, ready for the next part of the adventure to begin. Now all I needed was someone to meet me!

# Chapter Eight
# Close Encounters of the Bird Kind

Jilli

First impression on meeting Farmer Bird at the airport was, yippee someone smaller than me, has she escaped from the circus? And me being me, felt the need to mention it immediately.

I had read her book and was well aware of her past so I felt I should tread carefully initially until I could assess the situation, and see if the bravado was just a front. But almost immediately it became apparent that Janet was a very genuine person and I knew before we'd left the airport that she was on the level.

As we chatted and got to know each other I found she was happy to discuss openly all aspects of her life and more besides what was revealed in her book She came across as very intelligent and open minded and there was an instant bond.

We stopped on the way home for pizza and a glass of the local vino, so we had more time to relax and chat to get to know each other better, then went home to my house to go to bed.

The next morning Farmer Bird was up bright and early and had got through half a dozen cups of tea before I had even yawned. I dragged myself out of bed, as we only had one day in Italy to prepare for the Road Trip, so we had to get cracking.

Although she had not been abroad before and never driven on the 'wrong' side of the road, Janet was happy to have a go. So while my car was being given the once over by the local mechanic, she drove me around the town in a 'lend' car that should have been scrapped in 1987. Its only good point was that if she trashed it nobody would care.

The ignition was broken so it took two of us to get it started, and once we had it going we daren't turn it off. At first she struggled with changing gear and ended up winding the window down every time the car screamed for attention. After ten minutes she seemed to get the hang of it though and it wasn't long before she was driving like an Italian - down the middle of the road. There was a brief moment when I feared for my life, but this was an adventure and an experience so I had to chill out and give in to it.

I had been both fascinated and horrified by her story when I read her book, but now after meeting her I had so much respect and admiration for her. She has experienced some horrendous things and is clearly still recovering.

I only spent a week with her but I feel like I really got to know her and was amazed at her ability to retain a sense of humour, and not just any sense of humour - this woman is hysterical without trying. In some ways she reminds me of my mum, because like my mum she has the ability to make others laugh without trying and without knowing the effect she has on them.

Janet

I walked very slowly down the centre of the arrivals section at Bologna airport, looking for Jilli. I couldn't see any signs of anyone I recognised. The only picture I had seen of Jilli was that of her on the front of her book. I thought she'd look something like that, perhaps a bit older, but that should give me an idea. But I couldn't see anyone that looked like her. I knew she'd have her daughter Millie with her but of course I didn't know what her daughter looked like.

So I wandered on down until I got to the doors which led outside. I thought it was best not to start roaming round Italy on my own, unable to speak the language, so I sat down near the arrivals entrance and got my phone out. I typed out a text to Jilli saying I had arrived and was near the Arrivals doors.

As I sent it, I looked up and saw someone who I recognised from the picture as Jilli, with a young woman at her side, holding a large cardboard sign saying 'Farmer Bird'! We greeted each other and started to talk.

First impressions? Well I'd built up a picture in my mind of both Jilli and Tottie but quite often when you do that it never turns out to be as you imagine.

I thought Jilli would probably have changed a bit, or even a lot, from the picture I had seen, and wouldn't sound like I expected her to sound. But in actual fact she was exactly what I expected. She looked a little bit older than the picture on her book but the features were the same and when she spoke, it was in a very broad Yorkshire dialect and in no time at all we were chatting as if we had known each other for years.

Jilli seemed very nice, very welcoming. We went to find her car in the airport car park and she suggested we stop for a pizza on the way back to her house, which we did.

My first impression of Jilli's daughter was that she seemed nice and very clued up. She didn't speak unless I spoke to her first, perhaps a typical teenager. She was clearly fluent in Italian, which is obviously her first language, but also in English too. Very nice to have the ability to speak those two languages so well.

We had an excellent pizza which was so large each of us had to take half of it home to have the next day. Then off we went to Jilli's home. It was evening by now and getting dark so I couldn't see a great deal other than lights and shadows of mountains.

We drove for quite a distance up what seemed to be a very quiet road and arrived at Jilli's house. Jilli was very friendly, making me feel at home, perhaps a little bit free with the swearing but that actually made me feel very relaxed as she clearly wasn't trying to put on any airs and graces for me or trying to pretend she was something she wasn't. She was acting absolutely normally from the very second we met and that's great, I just felt completely at home.

In no time at all, strangely enough, not having seen any of the scenery since it was dark when I arrived, I immediately felt like I was in Yorkshire with someone I had known for years. There were no big surprises about Jilli, so far so good.

I woke up fairly early next morning to a very pleasant and picturesque landscape for my first day in Italy. There were no sounds from upstairs so I made myself a cup of tea and then wandered outside to have a look at Italy in the dawn. It was a bit misty outside and I couldn't see the top of the mountains which were obliterated by mist and cloud cover. From what I could see I was looking out onto a very impressive mountain, with a range of other smaller mountains running off to either side, and little villages and hamlets scattered in the valley amidst the trees at the foot of the mountains.

The mountain I was looking at, I later learned was Mount Cusna, the second highest peak in the northern Appenine region, very steep and remote. It has an altitude of just under seven thousand feet and the range of which it forms part is also known as 'The Dead Man' or 'The Giant' because of its appearance, as it look like a man lying down.

The peak contains a population of Alpine marmots, as well as herds of semi-wild horses that graze on its slope. The view of the mountain, immediately in front of Jilli's property, is quite breathtaking and inviting to those who want long walks, mountain climbs and natural, serene wilderness.

It was a very impressive area to wake up in, let alone live in, and I couldn't help but think that Jilli, for all her past trials and tribulations, was very lucky to live in such a beautiful place. I continued wandering about outside for a little while as there was still no sign of my hostess being up and about.

I had a look at Goat Cottage, a very nice place for glamping holidays. I think Jilli's done really well to do that conversion all herself, from a humble goat hut to a very cosy and comfortable glamour camping cabin. I had a look at the land she's got which has loads of potential for a little camping site, I would have thought.

I learned later from Jilli that in the area she's in they don't really seem to encourage people to come and do touristy things like camping. There were very few people walking about with rucksacks while I was there and I did notice the absence of camp sites and caravan sites.

Swings and roundabouts really, it makes the place far more isolated and pleasant to be in from my perspective, but Jilli wants to get a bit of business going with camping and glamping, although most of the tourists seem to head to Tuscany instead, which is not far away.

Having taken my fill of the views and the early morning mountain air, I returned to the kitchen and, needless to say, another cup of tea. I was already thoroughly enjoying my first day ever in Italy.

**later, via email:**

*Tottie: Really impressed that you two are getting on with the writing! Thought I'd be having to chase you with the big whip all the time. I'll keep sending you stuff as I edit it so you can see how it's going and add in or take out bits as you need to. Do you want .pdfs like this or Word .docx?*

*Jilli: Is this a PDF?*

*Tottie: This is a pdf. That's why at the end of the file name it says .pdf*

*Jilli: Fabulouso!*

**later, via email:**

*Jilli: Just been reading through Farmer Bird's stuff, really interesting and intelligent, but where the feck did she get this story about wild horses?*

*Tottie: I thought you lived there, Doris. Google is full of pictures of the brumbies on Monte Cusna. We need to know the Italian word for brumbies, to add local colour.*

*Jilli: WTF is a brumbie?*

*Tottie: <sigh> a wild horse, Doris. Brumbies down under, mustangs in the States, mesteño in Spanish, WTF are they called in Italy??*

*Jilli: Never been down under have I? Will look into it.*

*Janet: Well that does surprise me!!! A brumby is a short handled sweeping brush, very common in mountainous regions. When approached it can turn its bristles towards you and spit venomous bleach into your eyes. So - be careful out there!*

*Tottie: Not sure which of you has the greater need of the padded cell <sigh>*

*Janet: I haven't watched forty-five years of David Attenborough for nothing!*

# CLOSE ENCOUNTERS OF THE BIRD KIND

*Jilli: I asked my research team and Millie came up with 'cavalli selvaggi' but I think I would go with Tottie's version. feckin 'oss is a feckin 'oss and a wild 'oss is a feckin grumpy 'oss!*

Janet

On the first day of my brief stay in Italy, Jilli needed to take the car to the garage to sort out some minor repairs which she wanted to get done before we left so we didn't have any problems on the trip. We also thought it would be a good idea if I had a go at driving on the correct side of the road for Italy and France and in a left-hand drive car, for the first time, on the quieter roads around where Jilli lives, before we set off on the motorway the next day.

I thought I did quite well really, apart from the fact that my brain wouldn't allow my right hand to change gear – I kept reaching down with my left hand and getting hold of the window winder! I found it quite difficult to automatically get hold of the gear stick with my right hand, but I got to grips with it.

Jilli kept screaming and shouting 'not too close to the side' and 'move over, you're too close to the edge' but I think she was exaggerating, I think I was perfectly okay, apart from one tiny little lapse of concentration.

We'd gone down to the garage and the shops and coming back I was feeling quite confident. The road to Jilli's is pretty narrow and winding and there's not much traffic on it so I was quite relaxed until we came to a sharp blind bend. I was confidently driving in the middle of the road but coming the other way was another car - also confidently driving in the middle of the road!

That made Jilli jump a bit but I'm quite sure I had it all under control. And we missed the car – or he missed us, so that was all fine and we were all set for driving to France the next day.

On the way back from the garage we stopped at some local shops and Jilli took me into what I would call a café, which sold pastries, cakes and similar. She invited me to try a local speciality called Erbazzone, which is a type of pasty filled with spinach and Parmesan cheese. I didn't think it sounded particularly attractive, but am always willing to try new foodstuffs. It was absolutely delicious. I could have eaten another two or three, but it seemed a bit impolite to say so!

We returned home and Jilli set about making an evening meal for later – a nice chicken dish with lots of garlic, the recipe for which she had apparently pinched from Tottie! Jilli really was an excellent host, making sure the kettle was always on for the next cuppa, a bottle of wine at the ready in case I fancied a drink, and she constantly refused to let me wash up or do anything to help.

After a lovely meal in the evening we sat with a glass of wine, chatting just as though we'd known each other for years, and making plans for our next day's long drive to France to meet up with Tottie at her place.

# Chapter Nine
# Migrating Birds

Jilli and a bossy bitch (AKA pratnav)

Five o'clock in the morning, still dark and peeing down, me and Farmer Bird were raring to go (that's actually a lie) after a cup of tea. I locked up as Janet carried her case to the car. As usual she walked to the left hand side of the car, saw the steering wheel, shook her head and walked round to the other side. I took the first driving stint, while Farmer Bird was co-pilot, chief map reader and entertainments manager.

We of the positive attitude decided to give 'Pratnav' the benefit of the doubt and let her have her say, but before we had left the village I had already started an argument with her as she wanted to take us through the neighbours' farmyard. Yes it was the quickest way but if this was what she had planned for us I visualised us cutting across country through everyone's garden and getting arrested before daylight.

Boy did that bitch like the sound of her own voice!

'After 100 metres, keep straight on'.

What did she think we would do, somersaults?

'After 200 metres keep right'.

Nah, it's five in the morning, I'm going to drive on the wrong side of the road. I wonder what she'd say if I did?

The rain was pounding down on the roof of the car making Farmer Bird feel at home, as she lives in a caravan, but for me it was a bit noisy for that time in the morning and I could have happily gone back to bed for about five hours.

'What on earth's that?' Janet's sudden exclamation made me jump. I peered through the windscreen at the road in front of us. The tarmac appeared to be moving!

The road was a sea of frogs and I was struggling to try not to squash them. Often when we get torrential rain here in Italy the roads are literally covered in the little green monsters, not something I ever experienced in the UK, and it's awful to drive on as you are bound to kill a few, but what can you do, get out and move them all? There were hundreds and hundreds of them, and I was really trying to try not to squash them.

Then Farmer Bird suggested we gather them up and return them to their homeland, since for some reason the British have always called the French 'frogs'. It seemed like a good idea initially but given that the French eat frogs' legs, we decided to leave them to take their chances on the road. We had toyed with the idea of turning up at Tottie's wearing berets and a string of onions around our necks, which we could have managed, but turning up with a car load of frogs may have been a bit much.

The first few hours were fairly easy as I knew my way as far as Milano, but then Farmer Bird took the wheel and I wondered what the hell I'd got myself into. I had already told her that overtaking was illegal in Italy but I don't think she fell for it. I did on a couple of occasions give her permission to overtake but was gripping the edges of my seat when she did so. It was like the Whacky Races with Janette Krankie at the wheel!

The toll booths (or the man in the cupboard, as we renamed them) were a bit scary, as I had only ever encountered ones where you paid on the way out. So when we found one where we had to pay on the way in I got confused and thought we must have gone wrong somewhere. The fact of rarely leaving your own village was getting revenge on me, but we sorted it out and soon we were on our way again, flying down the autostrada, passing signs for Milano, then a couple of hours later signs for Paris.

**via text**

*Jilli: Are we going to Paris??*

*Tottie: You are not going to Paris. Do NOT go to Paris.*

*Jilli: There are signs saying Paris.*

*Tottie: The motorway goes to Paris, you do not. If you get to Paris, you have seriously gone wrong. Throw six to start again.*

Some people would have been excited at the prospect of visiting such places, but we just sailed on past with no interest in the cities that entice so many; we were eager to experience the green countryside of the Auvergne. After eight hours of driving, a fair few 'pee stops' and 'fuel-ups', we were happily anticipating a glass of wine in Tottie's garden in the late afternoon sun. But sadly 'Pratnav' had other ideas.

As we pulled into four lanes of traffic, in a busy city centre, with a big statue of some bloke on a horse, the bossy bitch announced (no doubt with a smile on her face): 'You have reached your destination.' As I stopped the car, Farmer Bird said: 'Is that Tottie on the horse?' and we both just laughed and laughed, hysterically.

Once she'd stopped crying with laughter, Farmer Bird got onto her fancy phone and I thought, great, she's finding a way to get us out of here to wherever Tots really does live. But no. Culture-vulture that she is, she was busily looking up who the man on the 'oss was and reading out all sorts of useless information about him to me.

He was some sort of revolting Gaul, I think she said, who had a big battle with the Romans and beat them. The only thing I wanted to battle with right now was a cup of tea at the very least, or, better still, a bottle of wine or two.

Starting to get a bit fed up, I suggested we got going and let Tottie tell us all about the Romans and the Gauls if and when we ever found our way to her house.

By now Farmer Bird and I were both busy hurling insults at the useless lying bitch of a pratnav, and arguing with each other about which one of us would get to stamp on the crappy little plastic box when we finally found somewhere to park up.

Then we realised that I had gone through a red light and had somehow managed to enter a city centre intersection with traffic coming at us from all directions and nowhere to go. So, like the foreigner in a strange land that I was, I just stopped the car and let them all drive around me, shaking their heads in disgust.

By this time we were bickering like a married couple, but realising how ridiculous the whole thing was, we collapsed into hysterical laughter, while trying to keep our eyes on the traffic behind us, so that we would know when to make our escape from the city of hell.

'Pull up, find a parking space,' shouted Farmer Bird, as if I knew exactly where I was. I responded with a number of swear words which quietened her for a few seconds, then the giggling started again and we were like a couple of giddy teenagers.

We came to the conclusion that Tottie was a fake alias on Facebook and that in reality she was a homeless bag lady living on the doorstep of a department store in this crappy city centre, and the whole thing had been a big joke to see if two unsuspecting numpties would really be daft enough to travel to a different country on a whim.

We were, we did!

We found a parking space, and rang said bag lady to tell

her what we thought of her 'countryside' only to be told that we had got off at the wrong exit and we needed to get back on the motorway.

Easy enough, you might think, but not in France, as they had closed the access road to the motorway and put up not one, but five diversions, so we experimented with all of them, before realising we were running out of fuel.

It was like being in a maze, so close but yet so far, no fuel, no way back onto the motorway and more importantly, no wine. To say we were a little peed off at this stage would be putting it mildly. But we had come this far, and we were nothing if not persistent. Also we knew Tottie had wine, so with this in mind and the goal in sight we decided, when in doubt, find an Ikea store and follow the arrows.

We eventually got back onto the motorway and, after another near death experience due to me looking at the fuel gauge instead of the road in front, we decided to be adults for a few minutes as we really needed to end this journey still breathing.

Twelve hours after leaving my house in Italy, we arrived at Tottie's grottage in France. But instead of stopping when we saw her standing at the side of the road waiting for us, we simply waved at her and drove straight past. We still had a sense of humour, though I don't know how.

But then we stopped and reversed back to where Tottie was waiting, looking a little bemused. Farmer Bird opened her car door and literally fell out onto the grass verge, as we all sighed with relief and had a hug.

Janet

Jilli and I were up early the day of the big road trip, and we were on the road by about five in the morning, thinking we'd try to arrive at Tottie's for around three o'clock in the afternoon. Jilli's daughter had very kindly set up the satnav for our trip.

Jilli insisted on calling it the pratnav and as it turned out, she was quite right!

We'd also got maps and directions which Jilli had printed off the internet, along with Tottie's instructions, so we were all set to go. What could possibly go wrong?

Jilli started off the driving. It was still dark and we had to go through all the streets of Italy, or so it seemed, to get to the motorway. The bulk of the trip really went very smoothly. We followed the satnav and at the same time checked with the directions we had, just to make sure. Jilli had no confidence in the satnav and I'd never used one before, but we followed it and we got onto the motorway and made our way through Italy.

As it got light I saw parts of Italy which were not perhaps quite as exciting as I had imagined as it was a rather flat area, though with mountains in the distance all around us. One of the first things I did notice was the lack of any animals anywhere in the fields but Jilli said that in that area of Italy they tend to keep cattle inside a lot of the time.

I found that a bit unusual having just come from Derbyshire where nearly every field has livestock of some description grazing. Here there were miles upon miles of fields with grass, crops of maize and all the usual signs of farming, but no livestock; no horses, no cattle, no sheep, no pigs, no animals at all: it seemed very strange.

Later Jilli nearly jumped out of her seat as I yelled, out of the blue: 'Look – cows! Brilliant'.

I don't think she'd ever known anyone be so pleased about seeing some cows grazing in a field.

After a few hours Jilli decided she'd risk it by letting me drive on the motorway so we changed over and drove through what I think were the Italian Alps, where it became very picturesque with the towering mountains on either side.

Then we passed into France and Jilli took over the driving for what should have been the last couple of hours of the trip.

# MIGRATING BIRDS

We chugged our way up through the French Alps, just as scenic as the Italian ones, with the mountains all around us.

We pulled into a service station around one o'clock in the afternoon and, with the sun shining brightly, decided to buy a snack and sit outside to relax for ten minutes. I think we both assumed that, being in France, the home of high quality chefs and cuisine, it would naturally follow that the sandwiches we purchased would be a cut above anything else we had experienced.

We sat at a picnic table on the grass at the side of the garage and stared at the mountains towering above us. As we unwrapped our food I pointed to a group of walkers setting off along a path leading up one of the mountains and asked: 'Shall we forget Tottie and go for a walk instead?' Jill didn't reply as she'd just bitten into her sandwich. I started eating mine. We chewed for a minute and then looked at each other, both pulling a face. The sandwiches were gross. Clearly the class of French cuisine did not extend to motorway garages/cafés. We returned to the car with a large bag of crisps to satisfy our hunger!

After we'd driven on for a bit, Jilli decided we needed some gas – her car is a liquid petroleum gas car – so we drove into a petrol station which sold LPG, or GPL as Tottie had told us it was called in France. Jilli asked if I'd ever filled a gas car before, which I hadn't, and it turned out she hadn't either as apparently in Italy it's against the law to fill up your own car with gas. It's considered too dangerous, so it's all attendant service.

That's clearly not the case in France. Perhaps it's not considered as dangerous or perhaps they like a good laugh if someone blows themselves up. So we pulled up at the pump and we both got out and managed to get the gas nozzle from the pump but the instructions were mainly in French and what English there was was very broken English, just as hard to read as the French. I tried to decipher the picture instructions, which were more my style, cartoon pictures of a man putting the nozzle in the car.

There were two levers on the nozzle and you had to push the nozzle into the receiving area on the car then press the levers in some sort of sequence which we couldn't work out. You had to do all that before you set the gas rolling on the pump itself. So we stood and we faffed about and I tried to instruct Jilli and that didn't work and she tried it herself and that didn't work. Between us we were getting absolutely nowhere.

Just to irritate us a bit more there was a man behind us waiting to fill up his car. He clearly knew how to do it but was leaning on his bonnet grinning smugly at these two women struggling to get this gas thing in. There was also an attendant inside who was grinning through the window, so clearly we were giving lots of people lots of amusement but not getting any gas.

Eventually, as there was a queue forming and we weren't getting any further, the attendant came out to help us. Of course he was speaking French and neither of us could understand his instructions about putting the gas nozzle in so he did it himself, but in such a way that it didn't show us what to do. He just put the gas nozzle in, set the gas rolling and walked away leaving us to it. But at least we got the gas.

At one point when Jilli was driving, all was going smoothly when suddenly there was a loud buzzing. Jilli slowed right down, unsure of the speed limit but convinced she must have been driving too fast as the Pratnav would buzz if you exceeded the speed limit. All the cars behind had to slow down as well. 'What's up?' I asked her, staring at the speedometer which had dropped to about ninety kilometres an hour.

'Pratnav,' she shouted, above the persistent buzzing. 'She says I'm going too fast'.

'Muppet,' I laughed, 'that's an email arriving on my phone!' As we drove, I asked Jilli about her friendship with Tottie, wondering how I would fit in with the two of them, who seemed to be such good friends already.

'How long have you known Tottie then?' Jilli seemed a bit confused by the question. 'Well, about the same length of time you have, I suppose. I think we all met on Authonomy at about the same time.' It was my turn to sound confused. 'So when was it you went to stay with her – you know, when you went camping?' 'What are you talking about? Are you sniffing gas fumes or something?' she asked me. 'I've never met Tottie, and I've certainly never been camping with her.' 'But I read about it in one of her 'Pig' books,' I said. 'How she was preparing for a visit by her best friend Jill and how she was planning to go camping with her'.

'Oh well, of course, there's only one person in the world Tottie knows called Jill, stands to reason,' Jilli laughed. 'That's the point of this trip – none of us have met before. Bloody hell, you're worse than Pratnav. So you thought me and Tottie were already best friends, and you STILL came to stay with us? What if we were a couple of weirdos planning some strange ritual? We might have imprisoned you......' Jilli stopped, suddenly very aware of my past record and what she was saying.

I waited a moment or two before I started laughing, as Jilli breathed an audible sigh of relief.

We carried on through France and it was just as Tottie had promised. As well as the picturesque scenery, the motorway itself was very quiet. In fact compared to the cramped and crowded British motorways this road (the A89) was a joy to be driving along. No roadworks, no hold-ups and comparatively little traffic.

So it wasn't hard travelling, and the satnav arrival time kept dropping down until it said we were only about forty minutes away from Tottie's house. We were still on the A89 and Tottie had said when we got off the motorway at the relevant junction to give her a ring to make sure we were heading in the right direction.

We carried on following the satnav and we just went on and on and on. Then it said take the next exit, which we thought was great. It was signposted to a place called Clermont-Ferrand so we took the exit in accordance with the satnav's instructions, and blindly followed the disembodied woman's voice as she took us down the road.

Gradually over the next half hour, the area that we were in became more and more built up, more town-like then more city-like. The road was getting busier and busier, there were more people about, then we were clearly entering the heart of the city itself, with buildings either side of us, people all around us, traffic everywhere.

I said to Jilli that something was clearly wrong as the satnav told us we had one minute to go and I thought Tottie lived in a really scenic, rural little place, very quiet, on a lane somewhere, with just one or two neighbours. I wondered if perhaps the satnav had got it wrong, although it had been right all the way along but at this rate Tottie must live only about one minute outside the city centre. It wasn't what I expected at all.

By now we were going down a hill into the city centre with the satnav saying we were something like forty seconds away from arriving so I suddenly thought perhaps Tots had been lying on all the contact we'd had with her so far on Facebook. Perhaps she was homeless, living on the streets of this city and she needed some food, or perhaps it was all a ruse to get us here with some gluten free biscuits for her.

Jilli started laughing and saying perhaps Tottie was a lady of ill repute living in one of the rather rough-looking flats we could see nearby. By this time we were tired and laughing almost hysterically. The satnav was still saying we were only seconds away so we decided we might as well follow it to see where it took us, then we would just have to phone Tots to see what had happened.

By now we were right in the middle of the city where there was a big square with a statue of some famous Frenchman on a horse. The satnav took us right up to the statue then said: 'You have reached your destination.' Jilli stopped the car and we both just laughed and laughed, hysterically.

We decided to try to stop somewhere a bit quieter, out of the traffic, to phone Tottie up, so Jilli set off down the street, with the satnav telling us constantly that we needed to turn round and we both kept shouting simultaneously at it to 'shut up!' Jilli drove on down this road and we had what felt like about seven lanes of traffic, a bus lane in one direction, a tramline which seemed to have priority over cars, a one way system in another direction and traffic just going mental all around us. In the middle of all this, without warning, Jilli suddenly stopped dead in the middle of the road and said: 'That light I've just come through, was it green?' I said I hadn't even noticed that she'd driven through a light, but she said all the traffic behind her had stopped, and all the traffic around us was revving up and going past us very close and pipping their horns at us. But we managed to get through it and pull up at the side of the road so I could phone Tottie.

At first I don't think she believed us when I said the name of the place where we were, but then when I mentioned the man on the horse statue, she delighted us by saying we were about sixty-five miles away from where she lived.

The next thing was to put instructions into the satnav to take us back to the A89 motorway from which we would travel back towards Lyon, then Tottie would give us the instructions once we found the correct turning off the A89.

Simple enough, or so it seemed. We put the A89 as our destination into the satnav and off we set, following the instructions, which took us out of the city towards the motorway. When we came to the first big roundabout we had to take the third exit but when we got to the exit it had all been taped off - there was a diversion, or a déviation, as they call it.

We had déviations one, two, three, four and five at these roundabouts.

We tried following deviation one but lost that and finished up on deviation two, which we followed for several miles, with absolutely no idea where we were. The satnav kept annoyingly saying 'you need to make a U-turn'. By this time we were getting quite tired and having little bouts of getting snappy with one another and getting irritated at the ludicrousness of the situation, but alternating with bouts of totally hysterical laughing when neither of us could speak and had tears rolling down our faces.

At the next roundabout Jilli turned off but we had managed to get ourselves onto deviation number four which we followed for quite a way until we realised it was actually leading us away from the motorway and back into the city centre.

So we found our way back onto deviation number two, which then turned into number five and oh were we having fun by now! But finally we found our way back onto the motorway and made it to the correct exit and from there, with Tottie's help on the phone, we found our way to her house.

As we arrived, tired, disgruntled at the satnav and very stiff and sore after about eleven and a half hours of driving, the last hour of which had been totally unnecessary, and we rounded a corner, Jilli said: 'There's Tottie, standing in the middle of the road. What shall we do?', so I said: 'Run her over and we'll go back to your place!' But of course she didn't.

Tottie

As soon as I answered the phone and heard a voice ask: 'Is that Madame Tottie?' I knew it was Farmer Bird. Not because I recognised the familiar burr of a Derbyshire accent, but rather because the voice swearing like a trooper in the background, telling the satnav to shut up and calling it a twatnav, just had to be Doris.

'We're in the middle of a big town, Tottie, the satnav says we've reached our destination but we can't see you. There's a big statue of a man on a horse, is that you?' My first reaction was that the Birds were playing a practical joke, pretending to be lost, as their last text message, nearly an hour before, had said they had just left the A89 motorway and would be with me in ten minutes.

Unless they were coming by helicopter rather than Fiat motorcar, that would have been an impossibility, so I'd replied saying it would take them longer. But their journey shouldn't have taken them through any towns of any size after leaving the motorway so I was a bit baffled as to where they could be.

'Which big town are you in?' I asked.

'No idea,' came Janet's helpful response. 'We can just see this man sitting on a horse.' Now the main man on horse statue subject round here is Vercingétorix, an important chap in these parts, who united the Gauls against the occupying Roman forces. There are a few statues of him in the region so this information wasn't helping me much with navigational aids. I asked for more detail.

'I can see a road called Rue Blatin,' said Farmer Bird, or rather ' Roo Blattin', but close enough!

'Whaaaaat???' was my incredulous response. 'You've gone sixty-odd miles in the wrong direction and passed not just the turn-off you should have taken but the one after it as well, which would have done at a pinch. You also passed within about twenty minutes of my house on your way. You need to find your way back out of the city onto the A89 and head back the way you've come, towards Lyon. Come off at the first exit for Thiers then phone me again and I'll guide you in from there.' I hate driving in and out of Clermont-Ferrand myself and I know it slightly. I was full of sympathy for two no doubt weary birds who had now been on the road for ten hours or more. They were about to get their first baptism of fire in the fun and games of driving in France – the dreaded *déviation*, diversion.

Various work was being carried out on the motorway and I knew there were diversions in place right where they needed to get back onto it. Unfortunately I did not know exactly where the diversions were nor where they went. I was just hoping they would be clearly marked and not the usual French method of putting different numbers for different directions, the explanations of which appeared in the local newspapers rather than on the overhead signs on the motorway.

**later, by text:**

*Jilli: Bonnie fecking Tyler!*

For those of you who don't know, one of singer Bonnie Tyler's biggest hits was called 'Lost in France'.

'Ooh la la la, Ooh la la la dance,' as the refrain of said song goes.

This was not looking good.

**via text:**

*Janet: Motorway junction closed – trying to find deviation route 2 to A89. About to run out of fuel but don't worry.*

By this time, my inquisitive neighbour was in her garden, doubtless wondering why I was capering about waving the mobile phone aloft trying to find a signal, as my place is in a reception black spot. I'd mentioned to her that I had visitors due to arrive, from England and Italy, and she was all agog to find out what was going on.

She was as gobsmacked as I was to hear the satnav had taken them so far out of their way and abandoned them, and full of commiserations for their plight, knowing of the many diversions in place.

**via text:**

*Tottie: Where are you now?*

*Jilli: Ikea.*

I relayed this information to my neighbour and we both nodded in agreement. Our intrepid lost birds were at least now heading back in the right direction. The trouble was, as they got nearer to me, I knew we were all at grave risk of running out of mobile phone signal so I wouldn't be able to communicate with them.

It didn't help that, superficially at least, to a stranger, the two critical place names I needed them to look out for were quite similar in appearance written down, Augerolles and Olliergues.

It turned out, too, that my definition of the top of a hill differed from theirs. I set them on their way from my nearest town of any size and told them to look out for a slip road at the top of a long hill and to come off there. They decided to take each and every tiny exit they passed on their way, so they did a scenic trip round all the lay-bys and parking places. There were lots of phone calls between us with clearer definitions of what precisely constituted the top of a hill.

Finally, some two hours behind schedule, I could hear the sound of a car coming up the road towards my house, a few moments after phoning through to the Birds with the last of my directions. I was standing at the side of the road where I couldn't possibly be missed.

A little blue Fiat came trundling around the bend and up the hill towards me, with two widely grinning women in the front – and promptly sailed on straight past me.

## Janet's Travel Notes – France
## Lyon

As we travelled through the French Alps we passed signs for Lyon, a city I'd heard of because they have a successful Rugby team and I much prefer watching Rugby League to watching soccer.

I searched my phone to find out information about Lyon, as it occurred to me yet again that I was passing so many places I would love to visit with no time to do so. Lyon has lots of architecture of interest and historical significance but I also searched to find if there were hiking trails through or around the City as I love the idea of long distance hiking.

I was disappointed to find the only hiking trail around Lyon totalled just thirteen miles and there didn't seem to be any link up to other trails across France. So I checked out parks and was interested to find 'The Golden Head Park' in Lyon. Its name comes from an old legend which says that a golden head of Christ is buried somewhere in the area on which the park was created. Apparently that's why the several entrance gates all contain the colour gold.

With a twenty-five acre lake, giant greenhouses, botanical and rose gardens, plus a number of differently themed statues and a zoological garden, this sounded like a park worth walking around. And with an area of one hundred and fifty acres, it would certainly be a good walk.

## Paris

When we passed a motorway exit signposted 'Paris' my heart gave a jump. Who'd have thought it, me travelling within spitting distance of Paris. This is such a well known romantic city and one which I would love to visit. Of course there was no time to spare on our current trip.

What would I like to see on a trip to Paris? There's all the obvious sights – the Eiffel Tower, Notre Dame Cathedral, Disneyland.

Well, perhaps not Disneyland!

One place I would like to see is the Picasso Museum. I read that it had been refurbished and reopened this summer (2014), and displays over five thousand paintings and sculptures by Pablo Picasso.

I've no knowledge of art but I do enjoy looking at paintings and I find some of them surprisingly moving. I cannot say I understand Picasso's work but I would like the opportunity to see his original paintings; to study them with an open mind and see if I feel differently.

Failing which there's always Disneyland!

Maybe I will return to France in the future and visit both Lyon and Paris.

# Chapter Ten
# Pecking Order

Jilli

First impression of Tottie in the flesh was that she was so young. I knew before we met how old she was and the numbers hadn't changed, but she just really surprised me. I didn't expect a little old dear, any more than I did with Janet, but nor did I expect such a lively vibrant bird. She must have put new batteries in before we arrived, I think.

Some people reach the age of sixty and seem to welcome old age, put on weight, buy a rocking chair and prepare to stagnate. And then there are the ones that think they are still forty and refuse to let the numbers dictate how they live. Tottie will probably still be a live wire in her nineties. I want to be like her when I grow up.

She went to a lot of effort to be a good host, and pulled it off; nothing was too much trouble. She even bought wine and she doesn't drink. She moved out of the house into a tent so that me and Farmer Bird could have our own space.

The house was a nice little French cottage with a fenced private garden. Once in the garden we were welcomed by Fleur, a beautiful dog with fantastic eyes and a lovely temperament, who was to be the centre of attention for most of our stay.

Tottie had one adjoining neighbour, which would not work

for me after living in the middle of a field for ten years, with only my own family, but I suppose it's nice if you live alone to have someone close by.

I don't know why but, I expected France to be more like Italy, the countryside was, to a certain extent but the houses and other buildings were very different. The cottage inside felt very English. The native drivers were just as bad as in Italy.

The first night I proudly told her how I'd cooked 'her' chicken recipe for Farmer Bird the evening before our departure, thinking she would see it as a nice gesture, but instead her response was, 'Bollocks, I've done that for tonight's meal.' Good job we liked it then!

She took us for long walks in the countryside to show off her beautiful surroundings, then fed us four course traditional Auvergnat meals with a selection of French cheeses, always served before the dessert in traditional style.

Tottie is as proud and excited about her part of France as I am about my part of Italy, so I could relate to it totally. The meals were served outside and when we occasionally got rain we just lifted the table into the 'dining tent' which was set up just outside the kitchen. This worked really well.

Given that only one week prior to our arrival Tottie had lost one of her best friends very suddenly (Ci the dog) I was really surprised she had agreed to go ahead with the get-together. I expected her to be a little quiet and have periods of sneaking off to be by herself, but in actual fact us being there took so much of her time and energy she was probably compensated by company at a time when most of us would choose to be alone.

I am very sociable, and can party with most people but also really enjoy being alone. Maybe it's a writer thing, because I got the impression that the other two birds felt the same. I love it when people visit me but also like it when they leave and I can have my life back.

So I have to admit the prospect of being in someone else's house and company twenty-four hours a day for three days did scare me a bit. I wondered if I might need to escape the other two during the visit, but I found them both so easy to be with and we were all so honest with each other that if a problem had arisen I felt it would have been discussed and resolved.

We had our business meetings in the dining tent in the evenings, where we dissected each others' lives, and our own. It was very enlightening and the other two Birds gave me some good advice. Neither of them has ever been a mother, but both of them were like one to me on those nights. In between the bouts of hysterical laughter we did actually have some fairly serious conversations and naturally we all had an opinion on everything, not always the same.

Tottie

The car stopped a few metres up the road, then came reversing back towards me to park on the grass verge outside my house. Then two by now hysterically laughing women burst out of its doors, one on either side.

Janet, Farmer Bird, came towards me first and my immediate thought was: 'Blimey, she's small.' Then I realised she was literally doubled up laughing, although when she straightened up, she was not a lot bigger.

I was busy trying to work out how such a small woman could build the big and stunningly beautiful dry stone walls I'd seen pictures of on Facebook. Next minute we were engulfing each other in a big bear hug which felt so right, like old friends who hadn't seen one another in ages, although this was the first time any of us had met in real life.

The second thing which struck me was that she bore an uncanny resemblance to my late Auntie Ethel, the inventor of my pen-name of Tottie Limejuice. Not that she looked like her exactly but there was something there which was striking. Perhaps it was the wickedly twinkling blue eyes. Or maybe the fearless attitude which seemed to say: 'If you think I'm a pushover because of my size, you've clearly never seen a single Jack Russell terrier dispose of an entire barnful of rats.' Then I turned my attention to Jilli and again, it was like greeting someone I had known most of my life. We had two hugs, one in greeting and one because Jilli knew how much I was hurting from the recent loss of one of my dogs, although I warned her not to be nice to me or I might cry.

When she had heard of Ci's death, it was Jilli who contacted me privately to make sure I was still up to the visit or if I needed to be left in peace. I'd urged them both to come, sensing that what I would be needing most was some laughs and the company of people I had come to consider as friends, and also because we had a book to write and when it comes to writing, I click easily into professional mode.

I led the way into the garden, the two birds still laughing uproariously about their adventures on the way, both talking nineteen to the dozen, which was to be the pattern throughout the visit. They were both greeted rapturously by remaining dog, Fleur, who loves everyone unreservedly, and soon had both of them under the spell of her kohl-lined Bollywood eyes and licky, waggy personality.

Fleur doesn't speak English; I've always spoken French to my dogs who were both from a French refuge. Even if she did, I doubt she would have understood Jilli's excited squeals of 'ooooh, snooky bunny rabbit face' on meeting her.

I'd planned a nice leisurely afternoon tea, with a specially baked chocolate cake, gluten-free because of my dietary requirements, followed by a walk with Fleur round the village before supper. By now though we were already two hours behind the schedule I had mapped out to allow us time to eat a five-course meal and get down to the little town for the firework display, and it was clear that what the Birds were most in need of was alcohol.

Time to pop the cork on a bottle of bubbly and serve it with blackcurrant liqueur in that most classic of French apéritifs, a kir royal.

It also seemed that the only way to stop the flow of chatter and laughter from these two women was to occupy them with some food and drink to keep them intermittently quiet enough so I could observe them to see if they were what I had expected.

Mind you, I'm a good talker myself. In that respect I take after my Luxembourg granny who could talk all four legs off the proverbial donkey without drawing breath. I once went to a spiritualist church, purely out of curiosity. The medium singled me out and said she had someone who wanted to talk to me.

The medium kept trying to relay the messages but then pausing to 'listen' to this person. Eventually she said: 'Excuse me for saying this, but this lady does talk a lot, she's not giving me chance to speak.' Granny, to a T.

I knew Doris would have a broad Yorkshire accent as she even wrote in one. I sensed this was a person who would willingly go without so that a friend didn't have to. What surprised me was that beneath the brash exterior there was a certain vulnerability which I had not expected, an ability to be hurt, perhaps more than she realised herself.

She'd professed total unconcern at a couple of quite nasty personal attacks in public on a Facebook group we all frequented. Any writer who puts their life into print for all to see runs the risk of bad reviews. It's hard enough to live with those but when the criticism comes of the writer as a person, it can be particularly wounding.

Her ability to read the mood of others also showed a much deeper sensitivity than I had expected to find.

She was clearly barking mad, totally undaunted by the trials and tribulations brought on by a satnav which was obviously on prohibited substances or had a very warped sense of humour. I suspected any such natural disasters in life would be like water off a duck's back, but that certain things, especially coming from unexpected quarters, still had the ability to wound her.

As far as Janet went, I knew from reading her book that she had experienced some terrible things in her life, including a term in prison. She'd already said from the outset that no subject was off limits and that she didn't expect anyone to tread on eggshells around her. We quickly found that she meant it!

Doris and I would constantly make joking remarks about some of Farmer Bird's darker moments, which were received in the spirit in which they were made – the clumsy attempt of new friends to normalise events which were far outside the norm and to show support without sentiment.

I let them both talk – and drink – whilst I quietly went about my favourite sport of people watching. I hardly ever drink alcohol these days, the results of a very misspent youth, and I'd offered to drive us down to see the fireworks so the other two could enjoy a few glasses of wine.

As I watched them, one word leapt out at me – genuine. Although I had read both their books, and corresponded with both off and on for some time, I had no real way of knowing if they would be anything like I had imagined them. Yet I very quickly felt relaxed and at ease in their company and formed the strong conviction that these were two friends who told it like it was, without excuses or exaggeration, and I could take what they said with no pinches of salt necessary.

It was a good feeling which boded well for the duration of the visit.

Janet

It was very strange because I kept telling myself, right up to the point of meeting Tottie, to prepare myself for her not being quite as I expected. When you communicate with someone either by the post or by email, even if you see pictures of them, there's always something that you're not quite expecting, perhaps the tone of voice or something that isn't as you expect.

But as with Jilli, I have to say that Tottie was exactly as I expected, I didn't really spot anything that took my by surprise. She looked like the picture that I'd seen on Authonomy, she sounded well educated, her English voice is like someone brought up in Offerton, Cheshire, as I'd expect *(what have I just pressed on this thing – is it still recording? Sorry, I'm having a silly moment there)*.

Perhaps a little bit taller than I imagined, I don't know why, but really no great surprise! She was certainly as welcoming and friendly as I'd hoped.

As soon as we arrived she introduced us to Fleur, a lovely collie who welcomed us with a laughing mouth and wagging tail and made us feel every bit as welcome as Tottie. As I patted Fleur and marvelled at her stunningly beautiful eyes I pondered over whether to say anything about Ci. Should I stay silent or say how sorry I was to learn of his death? In the end I decided to say nothing - Tottie seemed genuinely happy to see us and perhaps the mention of Ci would throw a shadow over events.

Tottie showed us round her house and the adjoining the barn which she may one day do up. The house was – like Tottie herself – very much as I anticipated. Although there is a next door neighbour, Tottie's house is nicely situated, with privacy and beautiful views. She has refurbished it from the 'grotty cottage' that it was and I was very impressed. Her house has two bedrooms and she gave Jill and me a bedroom each, having decided to stay outside in her tent with Fleur.

There is a nice large garden and Fleur lost no time in showing us her racing skills as she hurtled across the lawn when a car passed down the nearby lane. Tottie also tried to introduce us to her two cats, Bibi and Her Royal Highness the Princess Freddie, known as HRH, which were sulking in the barn. Although we caught a glimpse of them they were not going to lower themselves to approach a couple of foreigners!

There was so much friendliness emanating from Tottie and

Fleur (if not the cats) that it was impossible not to feel one hundred per cent welcome.

It wasn't a great surprise that Jilli and I got the bedrooms but it did make me feel a bit guilty that I should be sleeping in a nice comfortable bedroom with all the best furniture and best bedding while Tottie was outside in a tent. But she assured us she often sleeps outside in the tent and I know she likes to do a lot of camping so I just accepted it with good grace.

I thought how lovely it was to have such nice things around me as, living in a caravan as I do, I haven't really got anything that you'd call nice. Tottie had given me a bedroom with a lovely bed and other nice antique furniture. It felt very strange walking around in the room, unpacking my case and hanging a few clothes up. There seemed to be so much room compared to my caravan where my bedroom is part of my living room and kitchen.

Although Tottie had joked about providing me with a hairy old horse blanket to sleep under there was no sign of that, just very high quality bed linen – all a cut above anything I have at home in my caravan.

The food was good too; throughout the stay Tottie cooked us some really nice food but we both felt a little bit guilty as she'd made some things specifically for us and couldn't eat them herself as they weren't gluten free. There we were stuffing our faces with all the goodies she'd put before us and there was she eating her own gluten free food. She let us taste a bit and we found she hadn't been exaggerating – it really does taste like cardboard.

There was some stuff that she made which was gluten free that was excellent; there was a chocolate pudding which was absolutely delicious and Tottie was able to join in and eat some of that. I think if I was forced to live on gluten free food I would end up living on that chocolate pudding. She also had a little sip of wine whilst me and Jilli downed it by the bottle, but enough said about that.

So a good trip, an eventual safe landing and a nice place to stay. From what I could see it was a lovely area, with a valley in front of us and mountains in the distance, or rather volcanoes, as Tottie told us they were, all fields and greenery, in a nice quiet spot, although Tottie's got one or two neighbours dotted around. It was all quite a relief to find Tottie really did live in a quiet, rural area surrounded by picturesque properties, fields and hedges, with mountain ranges in the distance, and not in a slightly grubby hovel in the middle of a city, which an hour earlier was seemingly a possibility!

# Chapter Eleven
# Twittering On

Jilli

When we finally arrived at Tottie Towers we practically fell out of the car. After the hugging and giggling we had a tour of the place and a fizzy wine to celebrate. It all felt a bit surreal, after the initial idea, the planning and the build up - it just amazed me that we had actually arrived.

After being awake since 4am, then stuck in a car for twelve hours I thought I may fall asleep as soon as I was allowed to rest but as it happened I came round and the fatigue lifted.

We were fed a fantastic meal then whisked off into the town to look around and watch the fireworks. I have to admit I have never been a fan of fireworks but decided not to mention it as I didn't want to offend and Tottie had obviously arranged it just for us!

But seriously, I was embarrassed at one point to actually find myself stood gazing up at the sky with my mouth wide open in amazement. To describe it as spectacular is a bit corny and predictable, also understated but I can't really find any other words. I was so impressed by the whole thing and really surprised because I enjoyed it so much. What a fantastic start to our get-together.

The other two found they had so much in common, both having bred horses and coming from virtually the same town, they found they knew the same people. They gabbled on but I didn't feel left out, it was actually nice as I was so knackered and sometimes, believe it or not, I do need to just be quiet.

The first evening was very special and it made me so glad that we did it. This 'experiment' 'experience' will be something that I will always be glad I did and even so early on I knew it would leave me with lasting memories.

Tottie had given me the twin-bedded guest room which was lovely. I have a fetish for old furniture and she had some treasures, but one thing that caused a problem was that on the spare bed there was a life size cuddly sheep dog toy and every single time I opened the bedroom door it took me by surprise all over again, literally made me jump repeatedly. It was very life-like and I expected the bugger to bark, so I made myself a sign and put it in my bedroom door - 'Beware of the dog!' The other two thought I was nuts but it seemed to work.

After such a long day and exciting evening I fell into bed like a zombie and was just at that delicious place where you are so close to sleep when I heard Farmer Bird shouting me from the bathroom, in what seemed like a panicked voice. I imagined that she must have broken something and didn't want to disturb Tottie in the tent so was hoping I could help.

Turns out the only thing she had broken was my feckin' sleep, and it wasn't panic in her voice but mischief. After grovelling around in the dark to find the light and dragging myself out of bed, I stumbled onto the landing to find her with a big grin on her face having a chat with a spider the size of a small kitten. Whilst I am not afraid of spiders I am aware that most of us sleep with our mouths open and I had eaten enough for one night so asked her to evict it, which I think she did.

The next morning I woke feeling refreshed and rested and looked forward to the next adventure. Obviously by the time I got downstairs Farmer Bird had been out, ploughed a field and built four walls. Well, she'd been for a nosey around the village at least, and made me feel like I should have been up hours ago; does that woman never sleep? It was the same at my place, she had actually drunk six cups of tea before I had got the sleep out of my eyes.

I was disappointed to find that Tottie drinks 'monkey milk' (UHT); no good cup of tea can come from this mucky stuff, but she did redeem herself later by taking us to a farm and getting 'proper' milk from a 'proper' cow, much to Farmer Bird's delight. Between them they had a nice long chat about farming, cows, milk, and walls while I just listened in and picked up bits of it as some French words are similar to Italian.

We went for a lovely walk in the forest where hidden away was a beautiful château. I would have loved to get inside for a proper nosy, but apparently I would need a fiancé for that. It was a perfect wedding venue, wasted on us three but still it was a beautiful spot. We upset the resident cat and were escorted off the premises by said feline. Clearly he knew we would not be making a booking!

We were very lucky with the weather, we managed to eat outside most of the time and when it turned cold we moved into the 'dining tent' which was like a poor person's conservatory, though much nicer as you don't get a load of windows to clean.

When the other two were out of earshot (or so I thought) I tried a bit of my 'Delboy' French on Fleur the dog. She was very impressed and responded with a lick and a cuddle. I decided not to try it on any of the locals in case I got the same response.

The giggles continued for pretty much the whole trip but one that particularly stayed with me was when we were in the car and Tottie as ever was trying to share her knowledge of the French language.

She was just saying: 'Now the French word for magnet is....' when a huge truck came around the corner on our side of the road and missed us by millimetres.

'SHIT!' she shrilled, which naturally had us all in tears

within seconds. No idea how we managed to stay on the road to be honest, but a guy parked in the lay-by on his phone was stunned to see an Italian car go past with three hysterical women inside crying and howling. I felt like we should go back and apologise but I can't speak a word of French unless conversing with the dog.

'Mange tout, petit pois!' as Del Boy would say, in 'Only Fools and Horses'.

And for the rest of the trip every time one of us needed to use the 'S' word we said 'magnet' instead.

One such 'Magnet moment' was when we went on a dog walk later that day and had to witness a three stone bloke trying to control a six stone Rottweiler. That was particularly funny as it was like watching someone water-skiing across grass, but it ended well and nobody died!

Despite our ages and our lack of potential husbands this whole thing felt like a hen party. We ate, drank, and laughed until we hurt, it was so good for all of us. My only concern was that when me and Farmer Bird left, would French Bird go down with a thump? At some point the grief was going to catch up with her and I was surprised that she hadn't let some of it out. It worried me but I didn't want to spoil things and so far so good, so I thought it best to let her do it her way.

The next day we went to the famous soap factory that Tottie had already told us so much about. This was something I was looking forward to as Tottie had sent me soap from there before as a present and although I don't normally spend money I figured I could spoil myself this once.

It has to be said that Farmer Bird is very inquisitive, which is all well and good but left to her own devises we would still be in France three weeks later. She bombarded the 'Soap lady' with questions and we had to practically drag her out of the shop as the bakery was about to close and we needed proper bread for our picnic so we didn't have to share Tottie's cardboard.

It was one of the things that I'd noticed about Farmer Bird quite early on in our friendship, she craved knowledge and would ask anyone anything, which I found fascinating. She had to useTottie as an interpreter in France to get her answers, of course, and there was never enough time to get all the information she wanted. I liked this about her, she was constantly learning and always interested in people and the things that surrounded her.

We got to the bakery in time and set off up the mountain to do our walk and picnic. Down in the village it was sunny and reasonably warm but when we reached our destination it was like being on top of Everest in winter, or so I imagined.

When we arrived I jumped out of the car baguette in hand like a scene from ''Allo 'Allo' ready for the picnic, Tottie let Farmer Bird and Fleur out of the back of the van, then locked it. Then both Birds just stood and looked at me with a confused look on their faces.

'Doris the baguette does not need to accompany us on the walk', sighed Tottie. Well, I was thinking it was far too cold to walk and that maybe we could just skip to the picnic, but it was not to be, first I had to suffer a little.

I could and would have sulked under normal circumstances with normal friends that know me, but I knew these two Birds would both laugh at me and take the piss so I 'cringed and bared it.' It was feckin' freezing, I am not good with cold as I have bad circulation so I thought I may die before the picnic but surprisingly I survived and we had another taste of the beautiful French scenery. We eventually found some shelter and enjoyed our picnic before going back to Tottie's for yet another feeding fest and wine.

In and amongst all this we did actually sit down like grown ups to discuss the idea of writing about our experience, but not for long because we were only serious and sensible for about twenty minutes a day, then we opened another bottle of wine and it all dissolved into silliness again.

Tottie

I was really looking forward to showing off my home and surrounding area to my visitors. It's something I love doing, especially when, as I felt might be the case, these two would be receptive and interested to discover the differences between our three countries.

When I applied for French nationality, I had to take an exam in French at intermediate level and, as I like to throw myself one hundred percent into anything I tackle, I wanted to be sure I passed well above the required level. My French was passable. I'd done it at school to Advanced level, and generally spoke French to my Luxembourg family (my father's mother was from Luxembourg, hence never considering myself one hundred per cent British) so I got practice in whenever I met up with them. But I was a long way from being fluent and was always looking for ways to improve and to widen my vocabulary.

Language school lessons were prohibitively expensive, even more so than private one-to-one lessons, and my budget was limited. By chance I hit on a great way to learn. The local Tourist Boards are very active, with lots of guided walks and talks round many of the towns and villages, as well as wildlife and botany works. Best of all, some of them were free, and all of them were easily affordable. I signed up for all of them!

As a result, I'd learned all sort of fascinating stuff about my new local area, its history and heritage, its flora and fauna, and I loved sharing the knowledge with visitors.

If the Auvergne has a disadvantage at all, it's that there are so many wonderful must-see sights that it is hard to pick just a few, especially as my visitors would only be with me for two and a half days. I ruled out some of the further afield attractions, thinking that after such a long journey to get here, they may have had enough of car travel for a bit.

Once my guests had had had chance to relax after their very

long journey, it was time to introduce them to some serious French food. I was looking forward to impressing them with the chicken with forty cloves of garlic. How was I to know that rob-dog Doris would decide to hijack the recipe I kindly sent her and make it for Farmer Bird the first night? That meant they both had to eat an awful lot of chicken and garlic in a short space of time. But the very cheek of it – with all the Italian dishes she boasts about, she had to nick a French recipe from me!

I think they were impressed by the starter, though. I'd gone for a simple yet delicious entrée of smoked magret de canard (filet of duck breast) on a simple salad of home-grown lettuce and beetroot with a honey Balsamic vinaigrette.

Then came the chicken dish, followed by a home-made palate cleanser of courgette, lime and mint sorbet, to prepare the way for the cheese board. The Auvergne is famous for its cheese so I'd picked a few local ones and included some goats' and ewes' cheese, as Janet had told me she hadn't tasted either of them.

Dessert was a simple crème brulée with raspberries from my kitchen garden. It's always served after the cheeses in this part of France.

It was wonderful that our local fête was on the evening of the guests' arrival. I couldn't wait to take them there to see the firework display. I could see from their faces when I mentioned it that they were imagining something in a field with a few sparklers, some Catherine wheels and maybe a Roman candle or a rocket or two. After all, I had stressed that I lived in a small commune, with just over eight hundred inhabitants in the main town and all its satellite villages between them.

After dinner, we piled back into Jilli's little Fiat, with me driving as I was the sober one, and Fleur, who hates fireworks, safely tucked up at home watching the X-Factor with the curtains and shutters closed.

My little local town of Olliergues is down in a steep river

valley and has a small but none the less impressive château perched on a rocky outcrop overlooking the town, the dominating feature as you go down the long winding road into the town. I actually parked the car at the top of the hill, the best place from which to watch the firework display, and led my guests down the long flight of steps to the small town square and town hall at the bottom. There the funfair was in full swing but I couldn't persuade them onto the dodgems and after a big meal, none of us had room for the candy floss and brightly coloured sweets on sale.

We had a walk around the narrow cobbled streets and I pointed out some of the interesting architectural features, including the oldest house in the town, a former weaver's house, as the town developed round hemp production for making sails for the navy. My visitors seemed genuinely interested, I didn't detect eyes glazing over, and considering they had been up since five that morning, there were no signs of stifled yawns either.

I showed them the River Dore, fast flowing and essential for the paper mills along its valley, and straddled by a quirky medieval packhorse bridge, now only supporting pedestrian traffic and superseded by a road bridge for modern traffic. Doris had already said she wasn't interested in church or castle architecture so we merely walked past both, then I tested their historical knowledge by showing them a half-timbered house much smaller at ground floor level than the upper storeys.

I suspected Janet would guess the reason why it was built that way, if she didn't actually know it. She and I had grown up near a famous house in Cheshire called Seventeen Windows, which allegedly had some of its windows bricked up to avoid a Window Tax which was introduced. She did guess it, too – property tax was paid based on the size of houses at ground floor level, so the rich merchant who owned it had saved himself money by having it built out as it went up.

Then we climbed back up the long flight of steps to find

ourselves a good spot high up above the town, directly opposite the château, waiting for the fireworks to begin. In true French style, they did so with a spectacular bang and flurry of coloured flame cascading out of the night sky, exploding as it went into even more intricate kaleidoscopes of colour.

The looks on the faces of my guests as they watched the spectacle was simply priceless. It clearly far exceeded any expectation they had, with nothing so mundane as sparklers or Catherine wheels in sight. By now I was used to the extravagance of French firework displays but even I had to concede this was the best yet for the little town.

We were all totally transfixed by one particular firework which started off like many of the others, with a whoosh and a bang and falling coloured stars. But then it morphed into something totally extraordinary, with tiny parachutes falling out of the sky, bringing with them yet more colours and more shooting stars.

It was hard to imagine what could possibly top that but each rocket seemed to shoot higher, spitting out yet more brightly coloured rain of fire, with crackling and spitting flashes of green and gold, before a tremendous climax of the biggest and loudest one of all.

Then the town lights, which had all been dimmed for the display, came back on, the noise and lights of the funfair started up again, and it was time for us to head back to my grottage for a nightcap and beds which must by now have been very welcome sights for my weary travellers.

Janet

After settling in at Tottie's and having a lovely meal which wouldn't have been out of place in a high class restaurant, she took us to her local town, Olliergues, and showed us round the streets and the shops. I was boring both Tottie and Jilli with my questions about buildings and stone and how things are built there.

Olliergues is a very pretty little town built on different levels, with tiny narrow streets in between the houses and shops and buildings. There was an old pack-horse bridge, with the river Dorc underneath and I was particularly interested in some of the buildings which were built so as to be wider at the top than the bottom, which I understand was a way of reducing a tax levied on the area of the ground floor.

Our walk around the town was followed by a quite stunning firework display. I knew that Tottie had been anxious for us to see the display and, having watched it, I could see why. It really was an excellent display and I was intrigued as I watched one particular set of fireworks which exploded into balls of light high up above the town and then – just as you thought it was finished – from out of one of the lights came a small parachute which gently brought the light down to earth.

I can honestly say I've never seen anything quite like that. Of course the experience may well have been enhanced by the number of glasses of wine Jilli and I had downed since arriving in France!

In the evening Tottie made us another nice meal. If the amount and quality of the food offered by a hostess is a measure of hospitality, then Tottie was fast becoming the most hospitable person I'd ever met, and this is someone who has a very restricted diet! We sat in a tent on her verandah, not the one she slept in, and then Jilli and I, who were now on about our fourth bottle of wine, started laughing at something really ridiculous and we got into the state where neither of us could speak for laughing.

Every time one of us tried to speak the other would start laughing, and that carried on for something like half an hour and with the noise we were making laughing, Tottie's neighbours must have wondered who on earth she had got staying and I think Tottie must have wondered what she had let herself in for as she stood in the kitchen cooking our meal while we were sat outside downing the wine and laughing.

I awoke quite early the next morning and, of course, made myself a cuppa. I had a stroll up the lane from Tottie's, wondering what I would do if someone stopped me and conversed in French. I had a chat with some Saler cows in a field at the side of the road and asked them if they moo in French. They had nothing to say. At the top of the hill was a rather pretty church and I had a quiet look around the churchyard and gravestones before returning to Tottie's for breakfast.

Later that morning we went for a stroll around Tottie's immediate neighbourhood and met one of her neighbours who very kindly took a picture of the three of us together with Fleur who came with us on all our walks. We visited a local wedding château where a young cat escorted us off the premises.

On the third day of our stay, I went for a stroll round the lanes by myself early in the morning and the three of us then visited the nearby church and it was fascinating to see the different style of building. Tottie told us that it's local custom that people don't take photographs around the churchyard where the graves are as it's considered an invasion of privacy, which I quite agree with.

I noticed on a lot of the gravestones the word 'Souvenir' and I asked Tottie about this specifically as I couldn't understand the other words and 'Souvenir' seem a little odd. Of course when she explained in that context the word meant 'Memory', it wasn't odd at all.

From there we went for a drive up to a mountain pass (the Col du Béal) from where Tottie hoped we might be able to see Mont Blanc. Although it's a good long way from there, when the conditions are right you can see Mont Blanc from the top, but unfortunately conditions were not good enough to see that far, although it was fine and sunny.

It was still a lovely walk out, but a strange change in temperature, because when we left Tottie's it was fairly warm and sunny but when we got to the top of the mountain it was absolutely bitterly cold and the wind really bit right into you.

We had a walk to see the views, followed by a little picnic by a building, to protect us from the force of the wind. Then we walked up to the top of the mountain where there was a wiggly wall with a plan on it showing everything we were looking at – what do you call those things, Tottie? (*Orientation table, Farmer Bird – Editor's note*).

Fleur accompanied us on our trip to the Col du Béal, travelling in Tottie's hippy van in her own dog accommodation in the back. Since there was only room for two in the front and since I qualify as being not much larger than Fleur, I was given the honour of sitting in the back of the van keeping Fleur company. The other two Birds told me it was an honour, although I'm not so sure.

One of the best bits of the day for me was when Tottie took us to a local farm where she can get fresh milk. We went one day but the lady who runs the farm had just sold the last of her milk, so we went back the next day and had a somewhat stilted conversation because I don't speak any French so Tottie had to be the translator.

It was a very interesting half hour or so because we chatted and then the lady showed us round the farmyard and took us to show us the cows in the field and to tell us something about them, and I told her about the type of cows I used to keep. This lady had lost her husband not so long ago and was running the farm on her own so had stopped keeping so many milk cows and had moved on to suckler cows which were a little bit less labour intensive.

I was fascinated as I used to keep a large herd of suckler cows and we spoke of the different breeds and their merits. At times like that I could see how it can be very frustrating for someone like me who can't speak another language. It would have been really nice to stand and converse with her myself, even though Tottie made an excellent job of translating. It's still difficult to hold a proper conversation when you're relying on translation and I found it very frustrating not to be able to speak even a little bit of French.

As a farmer all my life I could have happily wandered round this farm for hours talking to the owner and comparing notes, but that's totally impractical when you can't converse in the same language. But it was still a very enjoyable visit for me - and Jilli stood and patiently waited while we all gabbled on.

Tottie also took us to a small factory where they make soap with essential oils. We all had a walk round there, you can pick the soaps up and just sniff at them and pick out the ones you like. There were dozens of different types of soaps, there were even soaps scented with chocolate and they really smelled like chocolate. I expected to love those yet when I sniffed at them I didn't like the scent of the chocolate at all on the soap. There were lots I did like and I bought several bars of soap and two big blocks of a special type of soap.

The lady there was very helpful, she makes the soaps and mixes the oils to create new scents and perfumes from the oils herself. I was boring everyone again by asking questions about how someone can work constantly with essential oils like that without getting to the point where they don't get the benefit from them or have their senses dulled by the constant exposure to the scents. She seemed to think it actually has the opposite effect and you get more sensitive to the scents when you're constantly working with them. An excellent visit, very interesting and I brought lots of soaps back with me.

The next day came all too quickly. We packed our stuff up, said our goodbyes and set off on our way back. It didn't seem like three days, it was all going so fast and beginning to merge, I felt like I'd just arrived as we were leaving.

Tottie had made us feel extremely welcome. A very good host, she had plied us with very good food and drink. She showed us around and is clearly very well immersed into her life in France, the culture and the people and is very knowledgeable about the area. If you ask her anything about the area, the church, the buildings, the people, she can tell you all about them, and she's clearly very happy where she lives.

A very good time and unfortunately after just over two and a bit days it was time to leave, to set off, this time, hopefully, straight back to Italy without detouring round Clermont-Ferrand to see the man on the horse again.

Before we set off, Tottie took us to a petrol station where they had gas so we could fill up. Of course Jilli doesn't speak French either, we were entirely relying on Tottie when we had to speak to anyone. This time we managed to attach the nozzle to fill the car and that all went smoothly, so Jilli went trotting off to the booth to pay. She presumed she would just hand over the money, as we knew from the display how much it was, so while she did that I returned the gas nozzle to its holder in the pump.

A few moments later Jilli appeared in the doorway of the booth waving frantically and shouting: 'Tottie, Tottie, she's talking to me!' It was hilarious, especially when Tottie said: 'Well what do you expect her to do, bark?' It turned out that all the lady was trying to say was could we please replace the gas nozzle properly as I'd returned it to the pump back to front!

## Tottie's Tours

### Clermont-Ferrand

Farmer Bird turned out to be an absolute sponge for knowledge. She wanted to know everything about everything, about places she was visiting, even about places whose names she had spotted just driving past.

Luckily for her, I'm very enthusiastic about my adoptive country and I love to find things out about it, especially my local area. I'm also fairly adept at internet research so what I didn't already know I was soon able to find out for her.

It wasn't long after the Birds' arrival before Farmer Bird was bombarding me with questions, starting with wanting to know more about the infamous 'man on 'oss' statue they had encountered in the middle of Clermont-Ferrand, our regional capital.

He is Vercingétorix, a chieftain of the Arverni tribe after whom the region is named. He succeeded in uniting different branches of the Gauls and led them in revolt against the Roman forces towards the end of Caesar's Gallic wars.

His big victory was supposed to have taken place on a plateau near to a small town called Gergovie, although some local historians dispute the actual site of the battle. There are monuments to him in various parts of France; the statue the Birds had seen in Place Jaude, Clermont-Ferrand, is a particularly fine one by Frédéric Bartholdi who also designed the Statue of Liberty.

Farmer Bird was fascinated: Jilli was tickled to hear that the town of Gergovie had previously been called Merdogne. I think most people know what 'merde' means in both French and Italian!

Clermont-Ferrand itself is a small city, with a population of not much more than 140,000, and less than half a million in its metropolitan area. It's also one of France's oldest cities and is probably best known as the home of Michelin, the famous tyre and map makers.

## Olliergues

When you show visitors round a place you really love, there's always that anxious moment when you think they may not 'get it' in the same way you do. I was so pleased that both of the Birds seemed to fall under the same spell which my little local town of Olliergues had cast over me.

I was glad, too, that I had done the free guided tour of the town on many occasions, in order to improve my French and my local knowledge, so that I could answer all of Farmer Bird's questions about the town and its history.

It's a small town, population eight hundred and forty-two (of which I am a proud one!) including outlying villages, thought to be one of the oldest towns in France and with many features from the Middle Ages still visible. It sits on an impressive meander of the River Dore, halfway between the French cutlery capital Thiers and the town of Ambert.

In the thirteenth century it was an important centre for the canvas trade, with a weekly market and artisan weavers in the area.

In modern times it's become something of an arts and crafts centre, with a manufacturer of pencils, a basket maker, a wood turner and, just outside, our famous soap manufacturer's retail outlet, where I always take my visitors.

Because of its situation on the river meander, it's a quirky little town, with narrow cobbled streets, and very few of them running in straight lines so it can be a little confusing to walk round initially.

It's also a great place to keep fit as the hills up and down to the valley in which it sits are very steep. Its château, from about the thirteenth century, sits high up on a rocky outcrop and is imposing, although not grand.

**Col du Béal**

The Col du Béal, where we had our picnic in the cold wind, is a pass in the Forez mountains at a height of 1390 metres.

The top is varied upland terrain and is a protected site, partly due to the wide variety of plants, including carnivorous ones. It's usually cut off to traffic by snow for some of the winter but is popular for various winter sports including snow-kiting and cross-country skiing.

Cyclists also love to tackle its long and arduous ascent of 8 – 9% in places. There are various different routes up, some longer than others. There are also some competitive cycling events up it.

There are many walks of various distances around the area and on a clear enough day the view from the top towards the Alps is stunning, with a glimpse of Mont Blanc in the far distance.

It's a good place to spot various interesting birds including raptors such as Montagu's Harriers, Honey Buzzards and my personal favourites, the Short-toed Eagles.

# Chapter Twelve
# Home to Roost

Jilli

On the day of our departure from Tottie's, me and Farmer Bird had a leisurely breakfast of chocolate croissants and brioche with home-made jam, while Tottie forced down the gluten free muck that her body insists on, then we packed the car. It felt like it was all over very quickly but we had made the most of our time together and like all holidays it had to end sometime.

Again my thoughts were with Tottie though, as with such a high after such a low then suddenly being alone again, I wondered how she would be. Silly me, she had a book to write, she'd be fine. And she wasn't completely alone, she still had the lovely Fleur.

After discussing the route home at length and planning how to get out of France without visiting that bloke on the horse again, I was confident (until we got to the end of the village) that we would be fine. If I could just find the motorway then I felt sure that all would be well.

It was, until Farmer Bird got behind the wheel again and tried to park the Punto in the back of an articulated lorry. I felt like I was in a remake of the Italian job.

We were tonning down the motorway feeling very proud of ourselves for not getting lost when suddenly I found myself struggling for a swear word - no really I was. My mouth was opening and closing like a goldfish gasping at death, but no sound was coming out, and she was stamping on the brakes like Micheal Flatley on drugs, as this big bastard pulled out in front of us and we had nowhere to go as we were boxed in. Amazingly Farmer Bird had it completely under control and I had to admit I was impressed (and grateful to be alive), so we lived to giggle again.

And giggle we did when it was my turn to drive. We'd left France for the Italian autostrada when some muppet was doing fifty in the third lane and I had go the long way round to overtake him. I suggested jokingly that Janet might want to show our disapproval by giving him an impolite hand signal. I turned towards her laughing, to see a shocked and offended face from the driver hogging the lane.

'You actually did it, didn't you?' I asked sheepishly.

'Well you told me to,' she responded, trying to shift the blame like a naughty child. Needless to say I hit the gas and sped off before he could catch us.

A bit further down the motorway, we both realised we needed a pee stop. We kept seeing signs for services but somehow always ended up turning off onto a different section before we ever reached one, and as time went on the situation became more and more desperate for both of us.

This was possibly the only part of the trip where there was no laughter, but neither of us could find humour in this situation and we both knew that laughter would have resulted in wet seats, so we concentrated on the road signs ahead. With each one we passed we knew it was only a matter of time, but at this point I really wasn't sure I would make it.

I have not peed my pants since I was about five years old, and had no intentions of doing it again until I was ninety-five, but it was close. Then we saw a service station and I broke the speed limit charging up the slip road, then parked like an Italian, screeching to a halt sideways, and jumped out leaving Farmer Bird to pull the handbrake on; I was only interested in saving myself.

I trotted across the car park and came back smiling a few minutes later, totally forgetting that Farmer Bird was in the same state. She rushed towards me and handed the car keys to me as she ran past like it was a relay race.

It was during this tense time, when we needed conversation to take our mind off the problem, we discovered that both of us had previously owned a Land Rover Defender. We both wished we had one that day, as the driver seat has a slider plate underneath that can be pulled out so you can see the road. I was so desperate to pee that had I been in a Land Rover I would have happily opened the seat and peed in transit.

Tottie

I couldn't suppress a feeling rather like relief as I waved my visitors on their way back to Italy, hopefully by a much more direct route than that by which they had come. Not that I hadn't enjoyed our time together – I had, enormously – but pressing on my mind the whole time had been the loss of my adored dog, Ci.

Perhaps the other birds had thought me rather heartless that I had gone ahead with the visit as planned. If they had, they had not fully understood that I have been a professional writer for much of my life, governed by the dreaded deadlines, and had learned a lesson about those the hard way.

My first editor, on a weekly newspaper in Greater Manchester, had been something of a Jekyll and Hyde character. Certainly alcohol-dependent if not a full-blown alcoholic, he had three states, between which he alternated: drunk, recovering from being drunk or busily getting drunk again. This made him extremely unpredictable as it was not always possible to tell at a glance which was his mood of the moment and how he would react in any given circumstance. His nickname within the office was Pissquick.

I was the only female in the newsroom and he had a reputation for disliking women reporters. His office was downstairs, the newsroom was upstairs. We'd hear him come lurching unsteadily up the stairs every day shortly after stop-tap at the local pub in the afternoon. Mine was the first desk he came to, which made it a precarious place to sit.

He could be quite nice to me sometimes. On occasion, if he caught me at an idle moment with nothing much to do, he'd smile benevolently and say I could go home. He had a reluctant soft spot for me ever since he discovered I knew more of his favourite Irish rebel songs than he did and press-ganged me into singing them all for him whenever the drink made him particularly maudlin. At other times he could go off on a total rant about me not being paid to sit idle and refuse to let me go home until I had conjured up a few feature articles out of thin air.

On one memorable Friday afternoon, after the hottest day since records began, he had allowed me to go home for the weekend without typing up the main lead story which was in my notebook – unheard of behaviour. The hot weather had jammed an important swing bridge over the Manchester Ship Canal, creating traffic chaos and long tail-backs of bad-tempered drivers. Ours being a weekly paper, the story would need to be written and subbed without fail on the Monday but I was given a reprieve until then.

They call it Sod's Law when something completely unpredictable comes out of left field to scupper the best laid plans of mice and men. In my case, it was a particularly dozy driver coming out of a side street and totally failing to see me pootling along towards her on my little Puch Maxi moped. I was certainly not speeding – those things could barely reach thirty miles an hour downhill with a following wind. The resulting collision sent me flying over the bonnet to continue my way, skidding and spinning along the road on my back, whilst the Puch ended its days crumpled under the front wing of the car.

Even as I was being bundled into an ambulance, I was asking someone to phone the office (this was long before the days of mobile phones) to tell them what had happened. Luckily I was not seriously injured although seeing how my helmet had been rent asunder, I realised I could have been. I was badly bruised, with a gash in my left knee requiring butterfly stitches, and the hospital insisted on giving me a tetanus booster, with what felt like a very blunt needle, despite me assuring them that I was fully up to date as I worked at a riding school most Saturdays.

The knee was rapidly swelling up like the proverbial balloon and fluid was building up, causing the uncomfortable feeling that my kneecap was being relocated. I couldn't bend the leg at all and walking was extremely difficult. Even in those pre-budget days, my injury was not considered sufficient to issue me with crutches.

My brother had to come in a taxi to collect me as at that time he did not drive and we both still lived in our parents' house. Trying to get into a classic high-floored black cab with a leg which didn't bend involved me holding onto the roof of the taxi and doing some sort of elaborate limbo dance to get inside.

It was afternoon before I got back home to lick my wounds. I rang the office, hoping for a word of sympathy at least from my editor. Unfortunately it was just after afternoon stop-tap and he was in the foulest of moods, with no main lead story for his front page. He ripped into me as if I had wilfully flung myself in front of the first passing car. He also made it abundantly clear that unless I phoned through the lead story before close of play that day, there would be no point in me going back to work even when I could walk again as there would be no job for me to go back to.

Lesson learned. He got his lead story, by the deadline, and I have never missed a deadline since. Even after major abdominal surgery for acute appendicitis – no wussy keyhole stuff for me, just a big scar across my abdomen – I was back at the keyboard in less than three days because I had demanding copywriting clients baying for delivery on deadline.

But now my visitors had gone, I'd put on my brave face, done my bit and we were on target to meet our punishing self-imposed deadline, as long as they managed to make it back to Italy and England to their respective keyboard and voice recorder. It was time for me to do my grieving, in private, which is how I prefer it. I had a whole river of pent-up tears still to cry before I could remotely think about settling down to write and edit.

I don't think the birds had believed me when I said I would have been sleeping in my tent anyway, even if they hadn't been visiting. They probably visualised me stripping the beds and reclaiming my own very comfortable bed indoors before they even made it to the motorway – assuming they did. But I really do love camping out and was determined to get as many nights under canvas (well, pretty upmarket rip-stop nylon actually) as I could before the wintry weather set in.

It was also somehow particularly soothing to cuddle up with Fleur in the tent and comfort one another in our sense of loss. Ci had always loved sleeping in the tent, and it was the warmth of his body lying against my back which sustained me through the coldest nights. Fleur was certainly missing his presence every bit as much as I was.

The other advantage of the tent whilst my visitors were with me was that, being at a distance from the house, they could not hear my nightly tears. Perhaps they thought me heartless that they had not seen me shed any. It's just something I needed to do in private Once my grieving had found its outlet, I would get back to my keyboard and put all the thoughts and memories down into some sort of order, before they simply evaporated from my increasingly senile brain.

Janet

We said our goodbyes outside Tottie's and Jilli and I set off on our, hopefully, ten hour return trip to Italy. Tottie had shown me a map of the local area and pointed out our route to the A89. For some reason she and Jilli seemed to think I could not only follow the local roads with all the French place names, most of which I couldn't even pronounce, but that I could commit it all to memory! Oh well, I thought, Clemont-Ferrand here we come - again! We travelled in silence for a few minutes and then I said to Jilli: 'I thought Tots would be really quite relieved to see the back of us – it's been a pretty intense few days – but she actually looked rather upset. Do you think she's ok?' 'She'll be alright. I think she's probably thinking more about Ci now that she's got rid of the company'.

'You're probably right. It's not going to be an easy few days. She's got to get his ashes back yet.' Jilli changed the subject as we turned left: 'You do know which way we're going, don't you?' 'Er, well, I think so. I clearly remember Tots saying "Follow the signs for ...." Now, what was it called? Something that ended in Table. Oh look, there's a sign for Noirétable. That must be it.' And so we began our scenic route to Noirétable. Strangely enough we drove to the A89 without any problems and even managed to turn in the right direction towards Lyon.

As we joined the motorway my thoughts turned again to Tottie. 'What do you think Tottie's doing now?' I asked Jilli.

'Probably fumigating her bed since you've slept in it!' was the instant reply.

The journey on the motorway was pretty uneventful. We negotiated the various tolls and, apart from an uncomfortable fifteen minute period when both Jilli and I were absolutely desperate for a toilet and couldn't see one on mile after mile of road, all went well. In the last few minutes of this uncomfortable time, the conversation went something like this:

Jilli: I really am bursting now – watch out for the toilet signs.

Janet: I'm already watching out for them. Can you stop going on about it – you're making me want to go now!

*a minute later ...*

Jilli: Bloody hell. Why are there no feckin' toilets?

Janet: Pull over into one of those little lay-by things – we can go at the side of the car.

Jilli: They're for emergencies only.

Janet: I can assure you this has just become an emergency. Pull into the next one.

Jilli: No way am I squatting at the side of the road with my knickers round my bloody ankles!

Janet: Why? No one's going to know you. If you keep going there's going to be a puddle.

Jilli: Oh, thank God. Look – toilets ahead, I'm pulling in. Now, here's the plan. The very second I stop I'm going to have to leap out and run – you stay with the car, stop the engine, if you get out keep the keys with you. Right, here we are, stopping now........

Jilli stopped the car, leaving me to wrench the handbrake on then she was out of the door and legging it to the toilets before I could object.

Half an hour later (no – we didn't spend that long in the Ladies, we stopped for a coffee break as well) we were on our way. As we drove and chatted I spotted a sign for Mont Blanc.

Janet: Look – Mont Blanc. That's the mountain Tots wanted us to see when she took us up the Col du Béal. Wow. Imagine being able to see it from there – that's one hell of a long way.

Jilli: Where you looking Bird? Isn't it that big mountain peak in the distance.

Janet: No – it's obviously that one on the left. It's got snow on top.

Jilli: They've all got snow on top. Muppet! I'm sure it's that one in the distance.

Janet: Why would they put a sign all the way up here if Mont Blanc is all the way over there?

We never did agree which was Mont Blanc even though it is the highest mountain in the Alps, rising 4,810m above sea level. A quick Google search showed me it is very popular for mountaineering, skiing, and snowboarding and the Mont Blanc tunnel runs beneath the mountain between France and Italy.

The remainder of the journey was uneventful and after about ten hours, we stopped for a pasta meal just before we got to Jilli's as she was a bit too tired to start cooking after the long drive. I had a tagliatelle with meat in a sauce which was absolutely delicious, and which was probably enhanced by the two jugs of wine, most of which I drank before eating the pasta.

We arrived home on the Tuesday night so we could have the Wednesday to rest and recover from the journey before I set off on my flight home on the Thursday. On the Wednesday I left Jilli to do some paperwork in the morning while I had a walk down the road from her house and along the flat bit at the bottom. I had intended to walk across to the little village on the mountainside that I could see from Jilli's house because it looks very close but in fact if you walked across it would probably take you all day.

It was a lovely walk, with the mountains all around. I found a little path and all the time I was walking, there was something skittering away from my feet. I got the impression it was something lizard-like, but it moved so fast I just could not see what it was. It was obviously something quite numerous as the movement and skittering was happening every few feet as I walked and the not knowing was becoming a little unnerving.

Every time I heard something I bent down to try to see what it was and on one occasion I just caught the briefest of glimpses of something, a browny-yellow colour. I thought perhaps snakes but I don't think snakes make that much noise, even though they can move fast.

Jilli later confirmed that small geckos are very common and are everywhere while you're walking. I just wished I could have seen one instead of just hearing the quick rustle around my feet.

*(Editor's note: I have just typed feckos from Janet's dictation – these two are a bad influence on me!)*

I walked along the track which led up the mountain and there were signs on the trees, either for walkers or perhaps for forestry workers, but I didn't have any codes to go off and the signs varied with different coloured stripes and sometimes a combination of colours, and little arrows pointing in different directions. I thought I better not go too far as I could easily get lost and I didn't really have suitable footwear, so after a nice stroll in the forest, I turned round and went back to the road.

**via Facebook:**

*Jilli: I've lost Farmer Bird!*

*Tottie: Well done, you win a coconut.*

*Jilli: No really, she went out for a walk ages ago and hasn't come back yet.*

*Tottie: Never fear, she will return. Just put the kettle on and start brewing some Yorkshire tea. As soon as she smells that, she'll be back.*

After I'd been walking about an hour or so, and was actually on my way back, I got a text message from Jilli saying: 'Where the feck are you?' She'd got a bit concerned as she thought I'd gone for ten or fifteen minutes and I'd been gone for an hour and a half so she was wondering whether to send a helicopter out.

I sent a message back to say I'd be there in ten minutes but the hill I had come down seemed an awful lot longer, not to mention steeper, going back up so it was actually about half an hour before I got back.

Jilli needed to get some groceries and she took me for a tour of her local town, Castelnovo ne' Monti. We walked around the centre, looking at the local shops, then Jilli took me to look at a local gun shop. Mmmm. A wicked sense of humour has this Italian bird!

**via text:**

> *Jilli: Feck Tottie, I just took Farmer bird into town for a look round and I can't get her out of the gun shop!*
>
> *Tottie: Yikes! Make sure they count everything before you leave and certainly before you let Farmer Bird anywhere near airport security!*

Jilli also pointed out a nearby geological formation called The Pietra di Bismantova. It has the shape of a narrow plateau, measuring one kilometre by two hundred and forty metres, with steep walls emerge three hundred metres as an isolated spur from the nearby hills. The top has an altitude of 1,047 metres above sea level, and it is very popular with rock-climbers, abseilers and other outdoor types.

Jilli told me the views from the top of this rock are absolutely stunning and promised if Tottie and I could be persuaded to go for a holiday, she would take us to the top. Me and Tots abseiling down a 1000m rockface! Super.

She then took me down to her local village and into the bar for a limoncello and then we had a nice meal together on the last evening and talked about the trip, and the book, about Tottie, and about Jilli's plans for Goat Cottage and a possible camping site. Jilli wants me to go to build some drystone walls around her property at some stage, maybe next year.

Then the following morning I packed up my things ready for the trip back. I had only a few Euros left which I gave to Jilli as you don't get full rate when you exchange them back. Later on the plane they were serving coffee so I asked if I could pay with sterling, which I could, but they gave me the change in Euros, so I ended up with a pocketful of Euros despite my efforts. Determined not to arrive home with any Euros, I bought a scratch card with them on the plane and of course won absolutely nothing.

There was a little bit of a hiccup in the airport before my flight which had me sweating under the collar. Tottie had given me an empty packet of some tablets she uses for Fleur who is frightened of thunder and the noise created by local shooting. They are perfectly legal but the name of the product begins with Canna so you can perhaps guess what they are made from. My dog Chico is exactly the same, he hates thunder or guns going off, anything like that, so Tottie gave me the empty packet so I would know what to order online.

You're supposed to have medication in sealable plastic bags and declare it but this was just an empty packet so I didn't think anything of it and just had the packet in my bag. There were also the bars of soap I had bought whilst visiting Tottie, two of which were not in the classic soap bar shape, they were just square blocks which were brown and white so they looked a bit like a couple of pieces of enamel or marble or something like that, only they were scented.

They were in a brown paper bag and I'd also got about half a dozen bars of ordinary-looking scented soap in another bag. My case went along the little conveyor belt whilst I was going through the X-ray machine. I went to get my case and the man asked if I would mind if he searched my case so I said that was fine, go ahead. But as he opened it I suddenly thought 'Oh dear, this empty packet of dog capsules, is that going to cause a problem?' He did actually stand and look at that but then he just put it back in the case. Then he picked up one of the brown paper bags which had my soaps in, the classic shaped ones, which he looked at then put back in my bag. Then he got the other bag of soap, opened it carefully, then just ripped the bag open without hesitation, spread it out, stepped back and just looked at it, almost as if it was a bomb about to go off.

He stared at the two blocks, then looked at me, then looked at the man who was sat at the end and they said something to one another in Italian, which of course, I didn't understand. Then he picked one of the blocks up and stared at it and sniffed at it, then he picked the second one up and did the same.

I was wondering if he thought I had hidden something in those two blocks then perfumed them and was trying to smuggle something through. It was making me sweat a bit! Then in the end he gingerly held up one of the blocks to the other man, who was busy typing away on his computer, then he turned back to me and said: 'Fine, madam, you can pack your bag up and go', so I did.

**by email**

*Janet: Jilli is sending you a story. Don't believe a word of it. As if I would.*

*Tottie: Hmmmm, now which of you two is more likely to tell me porky pies?? Heck, that's an impossible one to answer!*

*Janet: At Gate 18 all set to fly back to sanity.*

*Tottie: Bet you can't wait!*

*Janet: I seem to be sat on a BUS on the runway!!! Oh dear.*

*Jilli: Has the bus got wings? if not get off the fecker, it's not gonna take off!*

*Janet: No. Apparently we can't walk 100 metres. We had a bus ride from the boarding gate to the plane. 100 metres! Just taking off.*

*Jilli: Get outa my country, you soap trafficker!*

*Janet: HA. Got away with it.*

The flight back was much better as I'd picked a seat which did have a window so I really enjoyed flying over Italy and France to the coast as I could see everything, there was no mist or fog. I found it fascinating flying over the mountains, looking at the tiny villages at the base of the mountains which seemed to be very isolated places.

The view of the coast was exceptionally interesting from an aeroplane and as we flew over the sea, I was really looking forward to seeing the English coast to see how that looked, but as we neared land, the clouds set in and by the time we reached the coast I couldn't see a thing. It was just like flying above a cotton wool blanket, and it was all over the country. I never saw a thing of the UK as we flew in until about five minutes before we landed, so that was a bit of a disappointment.

My friend was there to meet me and I was whisked away home to an enthusiastic welcome from my dogs who'd been very well behaved and well looked after.

**by email**

*Janet: Back home now and the dogs are going mental. I got a video of it, I'll post it to Facebook, when I get a dongle signal.*

**Later ...**

*Janet: Ok. Well I've got a signal and my computer is trying to upload the video. Because it's a dongle it usually takes 30 minutes and sometimes fails but I'll perservere, or I may even persevere, and I will get it there!!!*

*Jilli: Or you could preserve it with a preservative or a condom.*

*Janet: Wot's a condom? Also on my Facebook page it says someone has poked me. Really? Do I do anything with that?*

*Jilli: Nearly spat my wine then. I poke nobody and ignore all incoming pokes.*

*Janet: I still don't know what poking means!!! Seriously I don't. I never felt anything when she did it! Hey ho. Still loading.*

*Jilli: Loading what though?*

*Janet: That's a good question. It's so long I've forgotten! And then you wonder why I don't do much of this. Hell's bells.*

## Janet's Travel Notes

**Italy**

There was so much to see and discover on my brief travels through Italy. Jilli clearly thought I was mad as I spent so much time on the internet, looking up the places we were passing through.

We travelled through Reggio Emilia which apparently is hexagonal shaped and has ancient walls and buildings dating back to the sixteenth and seventeenth centuries. On the outward journey, Jilli didn't seem to find that information as fascinating as I did at six o'clock in the morning.

She wasn't a lot more enthusiastic about my findings on Parma, but I was fascinated by my research. I found details of some stunning castles like Torrechiara, a Benedictine Abbey, built around 1450. I would love to have the time to see that.

I found a whole page of castles in the Duchy of Parma and Piacenza, some of which seemed to be private property, so presumably I wouldn't be able to just walk round. Jilli wasn't able to tell me much about them – as she pointed out, a single mum of three children had neither the time nor the funds to explore historical buildings.

I would love to make the time to visit, as I love looking at historical sites, including what my research told me was a magnificent Gothic Town Hall at Piacenza, which was named Placentia or Pleasant Place by the Romans.

My excitement at passing all the signs to Milano, or Milan, really highlighted the difference between Jilli and me. We both agreed on not being interested in the fashions and designs for which Milan is famous.

I've never had any interest at all in fashion or anything like that. Even when I worked in an office and I wore suits, skirts, heels etc – I could never get interested in clothes and changed into jeans and tee shirt at the earliest opportunity. I hate shopping for clothes.

Although my travel experience, until now, had been zero of course I had heard of Milan, because of their football team and fashion industry. I was fascinated by the fact that only a few weeks ago I had no plans to travel anywhere and now here I was zooming past places like Milan.

But whereas I would love to see the famous sights like Milan cathedral, the fifth largest cathedral in the world, Jilli said she would be more interested in going to the big antique fair, if only to look and drool.

I was immediately drawn to reading about Milan Cathedral. I love looking at very old buildings and this Cathedral took six centuries to build – it was started in 1386 and was not completed until1965. It's one of the oldest Christian buildings in Europe, built of brick with Candoglia marble.

As well as the Cathedral, there are lots of castles around Milan I would love to visit, like Castle Sforzesco, a tremendous fortress with various museums in the grounds with marvellous examples of medieval and renaissance art, furniture, tapestries, musical instruments, armaments, Roman art unearthed in Milan and Egyptian antiquities from the Greco-Roman period. It's just a few minutes north of Il Duomo and was once the home of a young Leonardo de Vinci. It sounded to me like a fascinating piece of the history of Italy.

Sadly, I had no time to see any of these intriguing cities or sights as our outbound schedule allowed for only one thing – getting to Tottie's in France in as short a time as possible. Then on the return trip there was the small matter of the plane I had to catch back home to reality and far away from all these tantalising places I would have liked to visit.

Maybe I can return to Italy and visit some of these sites – Jilli has a drystone wall to build and perhaps I can persuade her to take me to Milan in exchange for some building.

# Chapter Thirteen
# Birds of a Feather

Jilli

My first thoughts are that this was one of the best ideas I have ever had, and that I learned a lot from it. As a hermit who hates travel, I thought it would be hard to leave my comfort zone, but it wasn't, and it opened up new ideas.

My kids are grown, I am completely free, so maybe this bird need to spread her wings a bit further in the future. It opened my mind to new possibilities and this really surprised me.

I have been away for very short trips in the past and have always been homesick within hours. When I have to return to the UK I am always filled with dread. I know when I get there I will meet up with people I love and I will enjoy myself, but there is always something that makes me skip forward a week in my mind, so I can be back home where I belong.

The relief I feel afterwards when I am back in my own village is overwhelming. Strange that this trip didn't have that effect and I liked the feeling of freedom that it gave me. Bloody hell, I'll be buying luggage at this rate!

I came away from the 'Three Birds experience' feeling like it was all over far too quickly, and I would like to do it all again. I suppose I can relive it when the book's finished. But I feel like I want to stand at the side and see it all in slow motion so that I don't forget any of it. Maybe we should have had a video version, though the language might have shocked a few!

I go back in my mind to the very beginning when we were all finding our feet on a writers' website, putting our work out there for people to read and critique, and I wonder what the outcome would have been if we had formed a different trio. There were so many people on that site.

Somehow even before we met, we already knew each other well enough to have the confidence to do this. Janet, having never flown before just got on a plane like a teenager going to a party, seizing the adventure with no apprehension. I thought that was very brave. And Tottie opening her home to two people she'd never met at a time when she probably needed to be alone, or at least with people she was familiar with, not two complete strangers. Also brave.

The only brave thing I did was take a prehistoric car onto a motorway for eight hours, which actually turned into twelve the first time around, and I'm not sure if that was bravery or stupidity really - but nobody died.

I am, and always have been a happy person, even when times are hard or stuff gets to me I can usually find humour from somewhere, and do tend to laugh a lot with the hope that it's infectious, and I can make others laugh as well.

Like at my grandma's funeral when we walked into the crematorium and my brother said: 'It's bloody cold in here.' So I replied: 'Don't worry they'll be putting the fire on in a minute'.

We both walked down the aisle of the crematorium with tears running down our faces for all the wrong reasons!

But I don't think I have ever spent a whole week laughing, pretty much from waking up to going to bed, the whole day every day; we just had so much fun, laughing with each other, and at each other. That will always be my most memorable part of the trip.

The silliness, the smut, the way we all just seemed to run

off the same battery. We occasionally attempted a serious conversation but it wasn't long before someone hijacked it, and I remember at one point wondering why my stomach muscles were hurting.

We had joked that the book we were writing would make better reading if maybe we hadn't got on so well, but now having done it, I don't think so. It's certainly nicer to write positive stuff.

Tottie

If only I had thought to use the video function on my little camera to capture the look on Jilli's face in particular once the fireworks started in my local town! Never mind forty-something, she looked about ten, gazing up into the night sky in open-mouthed disbelief and admiration. It was a priceless moment which, although I didn't capture it on film, will remain alive in my memory as long as I have one.

That and Jilli's hilarious reaction to being spoken to in French at a French petrol station in the middle of France. Any time I am feeling low and need a good laugh, I only have to picture her rushing towards me, flapping her hands like an anxious chicken and shouting: 'Tottie, Tottie, she's talking to me,' and I immediately want to burst out laughing again.

My memories are quite hazy for much of the visit. It all swept past in something of a blur, especially as I was sleep-walking through my grief for much of the time, which passed so quickly.

I was struck by the companionable ease in each others' company into which we slipped so readily. It really was like catching up with old friends after a long absence, rather than meeting virtual strangers for the first time.

The eccentricity of sharing a picnic, four and a half thousand feet up a windswept mountain pass, remains one of the most vivid memories for me. I've never been all that

British, with only seventy-five per cent British genes, and since being Frogified (becoming naturalised French) I'm probably even less so than before. But could there be anything quite as British as sitting with our backs to the wall of a wooden hut, huddling against the wind, and making ourselves cups of tea from my trusty old steel flask?

Then there were those long evenings in the tent on the deck outside my grottage. The good company of new friends, long leisurely meals, good wine and endless talking. Discussing the whole crazy idea of writing a book together, in a punishingly short time-frame, just because we could. Sorting out Jilli's chaotic love life and hopefully setting her back on the right track. Persuading Farmer Bird that before embarking on the rigours of a solo walk on the Appalachian Trail, a doctor's visit to sort out the pains she was experiencing was probably a good idea.

There was a lot of laughter throughout the short visit. I managed to join in with some but not all. When you're the only sober one in any sized crowd it isn't always easy to get what is tickling the funny bone of others present, especially as some of it was of the 'you had to be there' type, from the adventures the other two had shared on the way. And of course my heart was not yet healed enough to laugh spontaneously at just anything.

One of the biggest laughs we all shared was our near-death experience with a lorry which led to the creation of a new French word! I was busy holding forth – pontificating, no doubt the other Birds would say – on the quaint peculiarities of the French language. I cited as an example the word for magnet, which is 'aimant', also the word for loving or affectionate, which I've always thought a charming use of words.

Unfortunately I never did quite get to finish my sentence as just as I said: 'The French word for magnet is … ' a huge lorry came round a tight bend in the very narrow road and seemed to be on a collision course straight for us, so I couldn't hold in the expletive 'Shit!' at the sight of it.

Jilli somehow managed to find a few millimetres of road in which to avoid what seemed like certain death whereupon we all collapsed into hysterical laughter at my faux pas and in relief at still being alive.

For the rest of the visit, whenever an expletive was called for, one or another of us would always shout: 'Magnet!' which quickly reduced us all to hysterical giggles.

The overall abiding memory for me has to be the delight of sharing my home and its surroundings with people who so obviously appreciated it almost as much as I did. Jilli, like me, is a country mouse, most at home in a quiet backwater with few people and no crowds.

Despite living in a field in Derbyshire, not the most populated part of Britain, Farmer Bird would obviously have loved more time to explore not just the delights of my rural idyll but also the big cities, like Paris and Milan, with their bright lights and teeming crowds.

I suspect Jilli and I were more kindred spirits in this respect than in any other. We'd be happy to drive her to the station, sort out her ticket and put her on the train, then the two of us would be off to a French vide grenier (attic sale) or the Italian equivalent, in search of trash to turn into treasure.

Janet

Now back in the UK, what lasting memories do I have of this whacky trip?

*Laughter*
The most enduring memory of my trip has to be the seemingly endless hours of side splitting laughter. Sometimes caused by hysteria, sometimes by a little too much wine, more often than not by the company I was in. It is many, many years since I have laughed so much and for so long and that was something I

did not expect. I am really beginning to feel like a normal human being again.

*The Giant Spider Incident*
After arriving at Tottie's and having a lovely meal, we retired for the night. Jilli and I to our bedrooms, Tottie outside to her tent! I unpacked and then walked across the landing to the bathroom to have a shower. As I opened the bathroom door a huge house spider strolled out and stood in front of me.

I like spiders and this was an enormous specimen. If you think of a small saucer and put legs on it – that's about the size of it. It didn't seem in a hurry to go anywhere, just stood in the doorway looking – well, spidery. Not one to keep surprises to myself I shouted to Jilli to come out of her room. Jilli rushed out clearly thinking there was something wrong and stopped dead as I pointed to the walking saucer. I think Jilli may well have just been dropping off to sleep and didn't really appreciate being invited to a preview of the film 'Arachnophobia'.

Assuring me she didn't mind spiders, she nevertheless insisted I put Napoleon out of the window. I offered to have him in my bedroom but Jilli had convinced herself that he had designs on her and that he would find his way into her bedroom during the night. Mind you he was probably big enough to open the door. I regretfully put Napoleon through the window onto the ledge outside and, without Jilli's knowledge, left the window slightly ajar so that he could climb back in.

*Tottie and the Rottie*
On the second day of our stay at Tottie's she took us a walk along the lanes around her home. With Fleur on a lead we strolled past some houses and Tottie mentioned that she needed to watch out for a neighbour's dog, a Rottweiler, which so far as she knew was friendly but which was a very large dog.

We continued down the lane when a young man appeared

round the corner with the Rottweiler on a lead. He climbed up the grass verge at the side to give us some room to walk past but, as we attempted to do so, the Rottie decided to get a little closer to Fleur. He set off and without too much effort simply pulled his owner right off his feet. In other circumstances the sight of the man lying on the floor trying to hold onto his dog would have been very funny, but for a few moments it looked as though we may have a serious situation developing.

In all fairness to the Rottie he was acting more like a daft pup than a vicious dog, but he was large and powerful and who can say what would have happened if he had managed to get right up to Fleur. The weight of his owner on the floor slowed the dog enough to enable Tottie to walk away with Fleur and we continued with our walk. The incident highlighted how easily problems can arise when someone has a powerful dog over which they have insufficient control.

*The village ovens*
Funny what things stick in your mind. Although time was very limited I did see some very interesting buildings and sights in both Italy and France, many of which I would like to not only see again but have time to explore properly. From all these though, one of the most likeable things I saw were the communal ovens in France where stone ovens, built at the side of the road, used to be used by people from the surrounding villages to bake their bread.

This struck me as an almost prehistoric ritual with friends and neighbours gathering together to meet, talk and produce that most basic of foodstuffs – bread. The ovens were also built of stone which naturally attracted me!

Tottie told me that some villages still use the communal ovens on occasion. I didn't see any of them in use but can imagine what a friendly and social event the baking of bread must become when they are used.

## TAKE THREE BIRDS

*Turkeyraptors.*

On my last day in Italy before reaching the end of this weird, wonderful and very surreal holiday Jilli and I called at at supermarket and, while Jilli walked around the shelves collecting some shopping I wandered along the fresh meat counter comparing the cuts of meat to what is on offer in England.

I was stopped in my tracks by a tray holding a leg joint of, what at first glance, appeared to be pork or lamb. It was in fact a turkey leg with a hock joint as large as a man's elbow! Having reared turkeys myself for over twenty years I could recognise the gargantuan size of this joint which must have come from a bird weighing well over thirty-five kilogrammes.

I couldn't take my eyes off it as I imagined turkeys the size of kangaroos roaming around Italy! The assistant behind the counter approached but then, as she saw me staring at the turkey leg and smiling, decided I was probably simple but harmless and retreated to the other end of the counter.

# Chapter Fourteen
# Pecking Things Over

Jilli

After taking Farmer Bird back to the airport, I found myself thrown back into normal life or 'Jilliville' as I call it, and actually it's a long way from normal. Pretty much as soon as she'd left, my mind was back on work, earning some money and sorting out my future, possibly due to some of the conversations that had taken place during the trip.

I was coming to the end of one of the messiest relationships I'd ever had, but also possibly the best I'd ever had. Before I met these two birds I just let it go on because he was one of the most considerate, affectionate, kind and loving men I had ever met. He gave me back the ability to trust and though I knew it was not meant to be, I was hanging on anyway.

A few days with a couple of 'grown-ups' put me on the right track and I left France having made a decision to finally end the relationship based on their advice and guidance. Unfortunately I didn't realise I'd fallen in love with him until I decided to end it.

But while there were the feelings of loss there were also feelings of relief because I knew once I did it, I would be able to move on, and I knew I was ready to find someone to settle down with. Who would have thought all I needed was a couple of strangers, a few bottles of wine and a thousand mile road trip to solve my problems?

I found Tottie to be very caring, and despite her protestations, she would have made a good mother, had she chosen that path. I could tell that just by watching her with animals. Also having read about the time she spent caring for her mother, I know the 'real' Tottie is a giver not a taker. Though she was a bit too motherly at times, like when all I really wanted was more wine!

I found Janet entertaining and interesting, her inquisitive nature at first made her seem almost childlike, but then her life experiences and intelligence would push forward her maturity and you see a conflict. I feel there is a lot more to her that I'd like to find out about.

I do think, though, from what she told us about her past she is far too trusting. She appears naive in some ways and tends to let others guide her, and she seems to have been guided and taken advantage of quite a lot. Whilst very observant of her surroundings she does not always see people how others do.

Getting to know the Birds on the web, and then meeting up in person was kind of an experiment as much as an adventure. Whilst all very different people with different lives, we clicked and had a really enjoyable week. I feel that we will remain friends and hope that there is a possibility in the future of meeting up again. I know Janet is desperate to come back to Italy and build a fortress around my farm, and I think by now even Tottie is tempted to try out Goat Cottage, as long as she can bring her dog.

Maybe me and Tottie could consider doing a trip to the UK together to visit Farmer Bird, and also the two of them could come out to Italy to visit me.

Either way I would like to keep in touch with both of them and hopefully meet up with them, either together or separately.

Tottie

Despite being thought of as a lucky number, three can also be a very tricky one. I had nothing but the greatest respect for Janet in leaping onto a plane for the first time to rush over to Italy then to France believing, as she did, that Jilli and I were already the best of friends and had met many times.

To a degree I had a certain amount of trepidation about being the last of the trio when we finally all met up. After all, Farmer Bird and Doris had already spent forty-eight hours in close proximity, and that was plenty of time to establish some sort of a relationship, good or bad.

If the two of them had really hit it off and become bezzy mates, there was a risk I would be something of a gooseberry, on the fringe of their friendship. If it had been hate at first sight, I could have been spending two and a half days refereeing at worst or managing a Cold War at best. And I'm not known for my diplomatic skills, it has to be said.

The main questions uppermost in my mind when we met were could I work with these two people to write a book and would I want to meet up with them again?

Writing together was bound to present a challenge. I write at a terrific rate which many people find punishing to keep up with. Janet had already confessed to not being a writer, although it was clear from her emails and interactions on the web that she certainly could write. But would Doris prove to be as scatterbrained in real life as she sometimes appeared online?

Initial impressions on that score? Well, after I'd carefully said don't trust GPS directions, whatever you do, our Doris completely ignored my carefully written instructions and blithely followed her pratnav into the heart of the city. So I wondered how easy it was going to be to keep her focused and on target.

Farmer Bird certainly liked to do her own thing. In fact, to use an agricultural expression, to plough her own furrow. She'd already shown that by her early morning exploratory walks, both at my house and at Jilli's in Italy. We'd both got used to waking up, finding her gone and discovering a note by the kettle saying she'd gone for a walk. Would that make her hard to keep on track?

Only time would tell on those scores. If anything would break up a beautiful friendship, me cracking the editorial whip could be the thing to do it.

So having spent just two and a half days with the Birds in the flesh, had they become my friends? Would I want to meet them again? Were they now on my Christmas card list?

No, absolutely not.

But only because I don't have a Christmas card list.

I would certainly like to keep in touch with both of them. I'd grown particularly fond of our Doris and her chaotic lifestyle. If I'd ever had a daughter, I'd have been pleased if she turned out the same – no nonsense, very practical, able to stand on her own two feet and tackle most things without complaining.

Although it has to be said the scatter-brained side of her might well drive me to commit dire deeds if I had to spend too much time in her company at once!

I had thought my travelling days were over but after the Birds had left, I found myself searching on the internet for trains to Jilli's part of Italy and mentally planning a trip. I had trusted friends who had previously babysat my cats who would willingly come and live in my home while I went away to look after Fleur. I could drive to Lyon airport, leave my van in the long-stay parking and jump on a fast train direct from the airport and with just one change of train, I could arrive at Modena for Jilli to collect me.

What of Farmer Bird Janet? She was great, I had nothing but admiration for her and all she had been through. I was astonished at how ingenuous she appeared, quite accepting and trusting of what we had said to her, enough to jump on her first plane and come and visit. She did seem surprisingly willing to believe what people told her, whereas I would have expected a much more suspicious nature, given her past history.

I also fervently hope she improves her navigational skills before tackling the Appalachian Trail. Every log pile I drove the Birds past she claimed to recognise and to have driven past before. But round here almost everyone has a log pile and the method of stacking is pretty universal. It was a bit the equivalent of saying: 'I've been here before, I recognise that black and white cow in the field.' I would like to meet up again with Farmer Bird. There was a but, however, and a big one, about her proposal that Jilli and I should go and visit her in England.

I don't do going back. I left the UK nearly eight years ago and have never been back there since, not even for a visit. France has become my home, I am well settled here and wasn't sure if England would prove too much of a culture shock after such a long time away.

If I were to contemplate a visit, it has to be said that Derbyshire, where Janet lives, has always been one of my favourite corners of the British Isles. Family weekends in my childhood were often spent discovering the Derbyshire Dales and the Peak District, and my distant memories are filled with endless picnics on Kinder Scout and Mam Tor.

The big problem was that I'd grown so accustomed to the wide open spaces of France and the very low population in the Auvergne in particular. The UK is less than half the surface area of France with very nearly the same population, which was mind-boggling to contemplate.

I was going to have to give it a lot of thought before I agreed to make a trip back to the land which had been my home for many years but which now seemed like more than a lifetime away.

Janet

When I first met Tottie and Jilli in person I was prepared to be surprised, even disappointed. I had got to know them both initially on social media sites and had built up an impression of two likeable, hard-working and friendly women who were not afraid to speak their mind. However, I'm old enough to realise that such impressions can be false and any friendship built up in those circumstances can soon crumble when you meet face to face and spend time in each other's company.

In this case I was wrong to be apprehensive. Jilli and Tottie were just as I imagined them, both in their appearance and also their warmth and friendliness. Jilli was so welcoming when I met her at Bologna Airport I felt I was meeting someone I had known for years. She swore quite a lot, but that made me feel at home and I joined in! She made sure I had everything I needed for my stay at her home and, although it was clear she was inundated with work during those few days, she never failed to make me feel at home and welcome, cooking meals and giving me guided tours, not to mention teaching me to drive – cheek! Similarly, Tottie was the perfect host. I felt welcome from the moment I stepped, or crawled, out of the car and so appreciated the care which she took to provide both of us with a few days to remember. She cooked excellent food and we wined and dined every day like kings – even though Tottie herself was limited by her gluten-free diet. The mood throughout our stay was one of laughter and enjoyment, despite the touch of sadness which was naturally present for Tottie as she had lost her beloved Ci only a few days before.

So my visit lived up to expectations and far beyond. Now, when I agreed to this slightly barmy trip, involving flying (never done it before) visiting Italy (first time) and France (first time), meeting and staying with two people I'd never met before, I agreed that I would be totally honest and up front about my feelings – even if I found myself hating either (or both, heaven forbid) of my hosts. So, dear Reader, we get to the interesting bit.

During the first couple of days in the company of the two

Birds, I started to wonder how on earth I was going to offer any negative comment at all about either of them, and how false it would sound to simply say these are two people I now consider friends; they are wonderful, generous and funny human beings. I began to feel that those adjectives were all I could come up with.

BUT ...

As the days passed I found there was one small irritation and it applied equally to both Birds. Several times I opened my mouth to speak out, only to realise that here I had my one and only negative comment – so I spent the last few days holding my tongue and clutching my comment to my chest in order to reveal it now.

As you will have gathered, Jilli has lived in Italy for the past ten years and it's obvious she loves her home, her friends and her life there. Although she has clearly had to work very hard to survive those years I feel she has the potential in her property and in her hard-working no-nonsense attitude to build a very successful future. Similarly Tottie has lived in France for nearly eight years and has immersed herself into the French culture and her local community. She has recently applied for and obtained French Nationality and she speaks French fluently. Her love for her home and the neighbourhood in which she lives shines out.

So. What's wrong with that I hear you say? Absolutely nothing at all. I believe these two Birds have both achieved what they have through hard work and diligence and I have to say they both live in beautiful areas where I personally would love to live. So. Where's the problem?

As the days of my holiday flew by I increasingly noticed that both my hosts regularly used phrases rubbishing the UK. I'm not referring to discussions about specifics –for example I know that Tottie experienced problems with the Health Services in the UK when caring for her mother and this is one of her reasons, I believe, for moving to France. I have to say I agree with many of her opinions about care of the elderly in the UK. I'm referring to generalisations from the two Birds such as calling Britain 'Shitey Blighty' and other similar expressions. It never seemed to occur to either of them that to someone who lives in the UK such generalised expressions can be mildly offensive. I would be the first to agree that the UK has a whole load of problems – but I think it's safe to say that about many countries. I doubt if anywhere is perfect. The UK has good points as well as bad, and I for one am proud to be British.

My final feelings are that I have achieved something very important for myself with this trip. Having had a few traumatic years in the recent past I now live very quietly on my own. I hate crowds and prefer my own company. You may think this conflicts with someone who has said she wants to visit cities such as Paris and is willing to go through airports and other crowded places.

I have come out of the last few years much, much stronger than I have ever been. I have learned how to deal with the problems I face when confronted with large crowds and in certain types of situations. I am determined to live my life to the full and take on anything and everything I want to. I am also determined to do all that I want to do, within of course the confines of money and ability.

This trip has proved to me that I can do exactly that and that I have nothing to fear and everything to enjoy.

So, having made (and probably just lost as a result of my earlier comments) two good friends, what of the future? I know that Jilli wants me to return to Italy to do some drystone walling. How I get walling tools and steel capped boots through customs is a problem for another day.

I have enjoyed my sudden and unexpected trip beyond anything I could have expected – mainly due to my hosts. I sincerely hope that this friendship will continue to blossom and next year – who knows.

# Chapter Fifteen
# Feathered Friends Forever?

Jilli

Well, after this I really don't think we can leave it there. I for one can't wait for the next chapter. So what about another meet or two? My mind is made up, I am definitely in.

This trip has changed me and I am going to start stepping outside my comfort zone a lot more. I do return to 'Shitey Blighty' occasionally. I have been back maybe eight times in ten years, but always to my home town to see friends, so going to visit Farmer Bird would be something completely different.

I went back to England earlier this year to do a book fair in the centre of Manchester, which turned out to be a total waste of time and money. It was badly organised in a dreadful venue which was really filthy and I sold only two books. Everything about it looked dirty after my clean country living here in Italy. I have organised similar things in Italy and sold fifty books in two hours from a tiny village bar. So have vowed to only do anything like that again if I have some input into the planning of the event.

Funny thing is that Farmer Bird booked the same event but backed out as she thought it was going to fall flat - had she gone then we would have already met. Pity I didn't have her intuition on that one. Tottie also warned me off – she thought it said it all when the venue was not even advertising the event on its own website. But I'd already booked my air fare and wasn't going to back out and, with my positive attitude, I was sure I could turn it around to my advantage.

I love Derbyshire where Farmer Bird lives and I am sure she will find a way to show us that England isn't all bad. I still love Yorkshire, if I'm honest. There are some beautiful places in the UK, it's just specific things about modern life in Britain that I went off.

It's over populated with over-worked, over stressed people and there is so much crime the place actually scares me now after living in a field on a mountain. There I can leave my door unlocked at night, my car key still in the ignition and lawnmowers, chainsaws and kids' bikes all just stored in an open shed.

In the past when the kids have left mobile phones/wallets/bags on the bus (as they do) everything always gets returned. One bus driver actually rang my son at work and said: 'I have your little sister's bag, can you meet me at the bus stop at the end of your road, so that I can return it?' That would probably never happen in the UK because there are too many people and they are all strangers.

One time when I was visiting the UK, my friend and I popped into a café. I put my handbag on a table, then went to order a drink and my friend grabbed the bag, thrust it into my hand and said: "You can't do that here, it could disappear.' I thought he was overreacting, but maybe I had been gone too long and had become complacent. I went to visit another friend in Leeds and was horrified to see that not only do people lock their doors, most people also have metal gates in front of them for extra protection. When did it get so scary?

I know that for my family moving to Italy was the right thing to do. My kids have had a very free and easy upbringing, being able to play out in the dark without fear, and going into the forests to explore, similar to my own childhood back in England forty-odd years ago. I think being a parent in the UK now must be a very hard job.

As well as the benefits to my children, for me personally the move abroad was the best decision I've ever taken. Italy has changed me and I see things very differently. My life here, despite my financial situation, is so much better than ten years ago back in England.

When I go back and visit friends, they don't understand my lifestyle and I don't understand theirs. They work long hours, come home and moan about their jobs then discuss what they are buying next. I find UK life very materialistic, it's a pattern that most people follow but don't even know about.

I was the same when I lived there. They just work to spend. Is retail therapy just something to kill the monotony? I have to wonder if they wouldn't be happier in smaller houses with fewer possessions, working part-time and actually having some hours every week to live life. We only have one go at it. It seems strange to spend most of it doing things they don't really want to do, to get something (money) that they don't really need. Well not in those quantities. But we are all different and this is normal to so many.

Rat race it certainly is - to me anyway.

The idea of the Birds coming here is great, I have it all sorted in my head, who sleeps where, what we will do, where we will go. My only sad thought is with Tottie's food intolerance I can't impress her with our local food, particularly not the pasta or pizza. Italians still think vegetarianism is an anti-social eating disorder so a gluten-free menu would probably be like asking them to cook a baby.

But I do have friends with a restaurant so nothing is impossible and I have time to plan and prepare. I love cooking and baking though so am already planning the menu. I shall send it to Tottie beforehand with a list of the ingredients to be sure I get it right.

She may have to bring the flour with her though as I don't trust Italian gluten free products any more. I bought her some biscuits and took them to France as a gift only to discover they had the dreaded 'poison' in that makes her ill. Just imagine if she'd eaten them without reading the packet. I already have two or three meals in mind that will be acceptable, so I'm not worried by this 'challenge' - she will be safe at my table.

While we were together we did touch on the idea of meeting again but nothing was planned, so now I have to see how the other two feel about it. I know Farmer Bird will be up for it, she has got the travel bug and will definitely come back to Italy to see more of the place.

But Tottie? I don't know, she seems very stuck where she is. I will definitely meet her again though because if Madame won't come to the mountains then I will just invite myself back there. I know where she lives (sort of) and Fleur already said I was welcome any time.

Tottie

It seems there are some advantages to getting older. I've been casting an eye over rail fares to Italy and to the UK, just out of curiosity, as I won't fly, and armed with an old grunters' rail card, there seem to be some bargains to be had. In fact it often works out cheaper than a flight, even if I could be persuaded to take one, although of course the train journey takes much longer.

That's not to say I have definitely decided to go and visit either of the other two Birds. I'm finding it harder and harder to leave the Auvergne the longer I live here, especially to take any journey which involves lots of people and traffic in close proximity.

I recently had an old friend staying and decided to take him into the centre of Clermont-Ferrand, to see the infamous statue of Vercingétorix. We were brave enough to undertake the adventure on the tramway. I hated every minute of it – so many people, crammed together, and standing room only. To top off his stay in the Auvergne I had to make the five-hour round trip to take him to the airport at Lyon and nearly went into meltdown with the unfamiliar traffic volume I encountered.

But I do love planning, so I've been exercising the little grey cells with all the possible ways of doing either of the journeys, should I ever decide to. And I do enjoy train travel, so it would be quite fun to jump on a train to Italy, or take the Eurostar back to the funny little island I left behind nearly eight years ago and have not visited since.

If I go to England by train, it would be retracing familiar steps that I've taken a few times with my brother, when we were first house-hunting in France together. He, like me, hates flying, so we always travelled by train, on the tilting Pendolino from our old home town of Stockport down to London, a red bus ride across the capital and then the Eurostar to Paris to catch a connecting train down to the Auvergne.

Stockport should be a fairly easy stop for Farmer Bird Janet to collect me, and Doris, if she travels with me, and from there, one possible route back to her Derbyshire home might even take us up the road where I grew up and spent nearly twenty years of my life. I'm not sure whether I would like that or not, as I don't normally do going back.

It would be interesting to see what Farmer Bird could show me that I haven't seen before as I know her particular area of Britain really quite well. I would certainly like to see some of the amazing walls she has built though. I've seen them in photos but I imagine the real thing would be quite stunning to see.

I still can't really imagine how someone of her small stature gets the top layers of stone into place unless she has mystic powers and can charm them into levitating into place by themselves!

Going back to England risks being more like time-travelling forwards, though, rather than stepping back in time. Here both the pace and the way of life are more like Britain of the 1950s and 60s, especially the low crime rate.

Not only do I seldom lock my house, I also often don't lock my van when I park it. On one memorable occasion I left it unlocked in a car park with my Macbook on the front seat and it was still there on my return. Like our Doris, I'm not a huge fan of Macs, but I was still relieved to find it untouched.

On another occasion when I took a friend into Clermont-Ferrand and we left the van at a park and ride to go in on the tram, he managed to leave his very expensive Smartphone in full view, on top of the dashboard in what is quite a rough city area. It was still there when we returned nearly three hours later.

From what friends tell me, many parts of Britain are not like that any more, and it's not just a rural area comparison. Before I left the UK for good, I lived in a very rural area of Lincolnshire, near Market Rasen. A local farmer, just back from the market with his cattle trailer still hitched up to his 4x4, was parked outside his farm, standing in the trailer to hose it clean. Some opportune thieves came by, jumped into the 4x4 and drove away, catapulting him out of the trailer, still with the hosepipe in his hand. I think I would feel very apprehensive indeed going back to Britain, and especially travelling on public transport.

Because it would be a new experience, I'm slightly more excited about the prospect of a trip to Italy to see Doris's place and Goat Cottage in particular.

I have been to Italy before, with the ex, on a camping trip, to a region called Trentino-Alto Adige, right in the north, bordering Switzerland and Austria. It's an attractive region, although I was a little disappointed to hear more German than Italian spoken in the region, as both are official languages. As we were living in Germany at the time, I really wanted something a bit more Italian!

I imagine Jilli's home and her lifestyle both to be quite similar to my own – just with more wine! I know from what she says and from what Farmer Bird found, that she is equally as settled and integrated into her new lifestyle as I am into mine.

If the two of us decide to travel back to the UK together to visit Farmer Bird, what a pair of country hicks we will appear to be! I've become so used to the French way of greeting everyone in every shop you go into – the normal thing is simply to say 'messieurs, dames' (gentlemen, ladies – it's a bit sexist!) as you go in, depending on numbers there are in there. I have visions of us getting some very strange looks if we did something similar in Janet's local Co-op shop!

Janet

So, is this strangely founded new friendship going to continue to grow? It appears to be a distinct possibility. Tottie has always, in the short time I have know her, been adamant that she doesn't travel and certainly has no intention of leaving France. Ever. Both she and Jilli have stressed that, having left Britain and settled in their new countries, they have no wish to return to 'Shitey Blighty'.

*Editor's note: It's only Doris who calls it Shitey Blighty, that's a Dorisism which I don't use!*

Recently I noticed a slight weakening in Tottie's stance as she has talked about the possibility of visiting Jilli in Italy, travelling there by train. How about taking that one step further and accompanying Jilli from Italy to Britain for a holiday in Derbyshire? Is there any possibility at all that I can persuade these foreigners back to British shores?

I would love to show Tottie and Jilli a really enjoyable time and send them back to their homes with a much improved vision of the country they have left.

In a way I can understand how both the Birds are apprehensive of returning to England after seeing how they live in their new countries. Where I live is very quiet and rural and, like the other two Birds, I leave my door open and never lock my van (it doesn't lock anyway!). I always leave my ignition key in and often leave personal belongings and tools in it but have never had anything stolen. However I do accept that a lot of Britain – especially the towns and cities – is overcrowded and that petty crime is often rife in those areas. I personally could never live in a town or city in this or any other country and I can see that some areas are bound to seem very busy and crowded to the other two Birds.

I understand the Birds' reticence even more after my visit to London in 2013. Co-author Helen and I went to the London Book Fair, a big trade fair at Earls Court, where well-known publishers from all over the world and other people in the trade have stalls. I had only been to London once before, when I was ten years old, and my parents took me to see The Horse of the Year Show.

I certainly noticed a change. It was a real shock to my system, the number of people, all apparently rushing from A to B, the noise and the frantic pace of life. On our first day we went to Earls Court on the Underground and I very nearly freaked out. Everyone was packed on the tube like sardines and as the doors closed I started to feel very panicky. We only had a short distance to travel luckily and I breathed a very big sigh of relief as we reached our station.

After that we decided to travel by bus. I was definitely wandering around like a country mouse and Helen, who is familiar with London, had to shepherd me around like a feeble old aunt. We stayed at a Travel Lodge which was on the bus route to Earls Court so that was quite handy.

The first evening as we travelled back from the Book Fair, we had to cross a busy road. I couldn't believe the volume of cars on the road. As there was a break in traffic we stepped off the pavement, Helen walking very briskly to the other side, me sauntering along admiring some of the buildings that towered above us. I heard Helen shout and glanced to the right where a double decker bus had swung sharply round the corner and was heading straight at me. Now in the Derbyshire village where I live any traffic, such as there is, does tend to slow down if you stand in the road, but clearly not in London. The bus simply drove straight at me and missed me by a couple of feet. I did speed up a bit then and caught up with Helen who was standing on the pavement open-mouthed.

'I don't believe you!' was all she said.

So, of course I understand the Birds' view of Britain, but the area where I live is very beautiful, very quiet and I am sure it can offer them an enjoyable break. Of course the obstacles to giving the other two Birds a holiday to remember (in a good way) are many, even if we do prise Tottie out of France.

Accommodation. Can I expect these two Birds to share my small caravan, complete with three dogs, in the middle of an oft-muddy field? Not really.

Tottie's diet. Her dietary requirements will need to be considered carefully as she can only eat gluten free produce and there is no way in the world I can match her culinary skills even if I had a decent kitchen to cook in. It wouldn't do to send them home with food poisoning. Not at all.

Entertainment. I could take the Birds on a drystone wall tour. No, that wouldn't do. Historic buildings? I don't think Jilli would find that particularly interesting. Stately homes? Again I don't think that's Jilli's cup of tea. Places of interest in Derbyshire? I know that Tottie has visited Derbyshire many times when she lived in Offerton so it would have to be something different to impress her and I have no idea whether Jilli has been to this area or not. Clearly they will be hard to impress.

Transport. I currently drive a twenty-year-old Caddy van which makes Jilli's old Fiat and Tottie's hippy van look like a couple of limousines. My van is on its third time round the clock, I pump all the tyres up once a week, the clutch slips and it looks, well, very shabby. Am I going to run the two Birds round in this rust-bucket, one in the front amongst the chocolate wrappers, the other hunched in the back between tyre pumps and cans of oil? I don't think that would do at all.

Clearly I'm going to have to wear my thinking cap quite a bit over the next few months, but I believe I can come up with accommodation, food, drink and entertainment which will knock their socks off – or their feathers! All I have to do is persuade them to make the trip.

**via email:**

*Jilli: This has all been just the most brilliant idea I've ever had. When are we going to do it again? We could write another book!*

*Tottie: <groan> Organising and editing you two muppets is like herding cats! I am going to need a very long break once it is finished.*

*Janet: I agree, it was great. I think you two are just very funny people. I really loved the the way we couldn't remain serious for more than ten minutes at a time, and the quick-fired humour once we all got together, with or without the wine.*

*Tottie: I would certainly have fired you two, pretty damned quick!*

*Janet: I'm friends with twenty-five letters of the alphabet. I don't know why!*

*Tottie: 'Course you are. keep taking the tablets.*

*Janet: WHY. I don't know WHY! Y. Get it? Ok. I'll take some more tablets.*

*Tottie: I'll send you some of Fleur's.*

*Janet: Ooohhh. Canna have some?*

*Tottie: I soapose so.*

*Jilli: Oh god, not one but two senile biddies on my hands! But seriously, I am starting to get really excited about the book now, can't wait till it goes out, and really looking forward to doing the next one.*

*Tottie: <grumble, grumble> If you don't stop pecking my head it will never get out!*

*Janet: Leave me alone now too. I'm researching Lyon as instructed. I know they live in Africa and eat antelope and such but I'm researching carefully to get my facts right.*

*Tottie: Stupid woman, they run a chain of coffee houses, surely you know that?*

*Janet: I think we need to turn Tottie off and then reboot her. I've got a very good steel toe-capped boot.*

*Jilli: If you two drank like I do you would both be dangerous!*

*Janet: So, you Birds. We're nearing the end of the book and it occurs to me that, once published, it brings our little tête à tête to an end. I know you two are in regular touch on Facebook and Twitter but I don't get on there that much and I wouldn't like to lose contact with you. I know Jilli wants me to do something with her wall next year and I'm certainly planning to do that. But here's another idea. Why don't you both come to Derbyshire and have a few days or a week here?*

*I can hear Tottie spluttering! I know you don't travel Tottie but I also note you've 'considered' the possibility of travelling to Jilli's in Italy. Come on - be brave. I would love for the three of us to meet up again and I can promise you a holiday you will enjoy! I will arrange proper accommodation (no I'm not going to ask you to sleep in my caravan with me and three dogs!). Plus I'll show you some sights you'll never forget! Take the challenge - come back to Britain!*

*Jilli: Ooh I smell an idea for another book, 'Recapturing the expats'?*

*Janet: Oh you've spotted the plan! Damn. It's a serious suggestion though - do you think you could get Tottie to Italy and then drag her here?*

*Jilli: Well, maybe if we kidnap her at gunpoint. I'll put the bag over her head, as you can't reach, then we can throw her in the back of her own van, lock her in the dog cage. I'll drive, you can keep your eye on her and squirt her with water if she misbehaves. Does this idea work for you, Farmer Bird?*

*Janet: You clearly haven't noticed that I've left Italy! Talk about making an impression. I left some weeks ago so you'll have to kidnap Tottie on your own. Just poison her with some biscuits which are not gluten free and when she's ill enough you can simply drag her onto a train and come here. Simples.*

## FEATHERED FRIENDS FOREVER

*Tottie: Right, you two, whilst you have been twittering on about the future, I have been plodding through the present with my red editor's pen and I think our great opus is finally finished. That only leaves one question – whose turn is it next time??*

# About the authors

Jilli Lime-Holt is the collective pen-name of writers Jill Pennington, author of The diary of a single parent abroad, Tottie Limejuice, author of the Sell the Pig series, and Janet Holt, co-author (with Helen Parker) of The Stranger In My Life.

If you would like to get in touch you can do so by:

Email: take3birds@gmail.com

Facebook:https://www.facebook.com/
www.Takethreebirds?fref=ts

Printed in Great Britain
by Amazon